# Christian Discipleship Made Simple

## June Payne

## Matthew Robert Payne

This book is copyrighted by Matthew Robert Payne. Copyright © 2018. All rights reserved.

Any part of this book can be photocopied, stored, or shared with anyone for the purposes of encouraging people. You are free to quote this book, use whole chapters of this book on blog posts, or use this book for any reason if it is to spread the message of Jesus with this world. No consent from the author is required of you.

Please visit http://personal-prophecy-today.com to sow into Matthew's writing ministry, to request a personal prophecy or life coaching, or to contact him.

Cover designed by akira007 at fiverr.com.

Edited by Lisa Thompson at www.writebylisa.com You can email Lisa at writebylisa@gmail.com for your editing needs.

All scripture is taken from the New King James Version unless otherwise indicated. Copyright © 1982 by Thomas Nelson, Inc. Used by permission. All rights reserved.

Jerusalem Bible: Scripture quotations marked JB are from *The Jerusalem Bible*, © 1966 by Darton, Longman & Todd, Ltd. and Doubleday, a division of Bantam Doubleday Dell Publishing Group, Inc. Reprinted by Permission.

Scripture quotations marked (NIV) are taken from the Holy Bible, New International Version®, NIV®. Copyright © 1973, 1978, 1984, 2011 by Biblica, Inc.™ Used by permission of Zondervan. All rights reserved worldwide. www.zondervan.com The "NIV" and "New International Version" are trademarks registered in the United States Patent and Trademark Office by Biblica, Inc.™

Scripture quotations marked (TLB) are taken from The Living Bible copyright © 1971. Used by permission of Tyndale House Publishers, Inc., Carol Stream, Illinois 60188. All rights reserved.

The opinions expressed by the author are not necessarily those of Christian Book Publishing USA,

Published by Christian Book Publishing USA,

Christian Book Publishing USA is committed to excellence in the publishing industry. Book design Copyright © 2018 by Christian Book Publishing USA. All rights reserved.

Paperback: 978-1-68411-511-2

Hardcover: 978-1-387-60178-3

# TABLE OF CONTENTS

ACKNOWLEDGEMENTS ................................................................ 6
BOOK DEDICATION ...................................................................... 8
AUTHOR'S HISTORY AND TESTIMONY ..................................... 10
LESSON 1: GOD HAS ALWAYS BEEN ......................................... 21
LESSON 2: PARADISE LOST AND CONDENSED GOSPEL MESSAGE ........................................................................................ 29
LESSON 3: PART 1 – SPIRIT, SOUL, AND BODY ....................... 41
LESSON 4: PART 2 - SPIRIT, SOUL, AND BODY ....................... 50
LESSON 5: JUSTICE, MERCY, TWO TYPES OF RIGHTEOUSNESS, AND THE ASSURANCE OF SALVATION ................ 57
LESSON 6: WATER BAPTISM, INFANT DEDICATION, AND HOLY COMMUNION ...................................................................... 66
LESSON 7: THE BIBLE AND FULFILLED OLD TESTAMENT PROPHECIES ................................................................................... 75
LESSON 8: FELLOWSHIP WITH GOD AND WITH OTHER BELIEVERS ...................................................................................... 86
LESSON 9: OLD TESTAMENT LAW VS. NEW TESTAMENT GRACE .............................................................................................. 97
LESSON 10: GOD WANTS TO FINANCIALLY BLESS US ......... 106
LESSON 11: LET YOUR LIGHT SHINE! ..................................... 117
LESSON 12: WHY DO BAD THINGS HAPPEN TO GOOD PEOPLE? ....................................................................................... 126
LESSON 13: A BRIEF SUMMARY OF THE OLD TESTAMENT .. 135
LESSON 14: A VERY BRIEF SUMMARY OF THE NEW TESTAMENT ................................................................................. 142
LESSON 15: END TIME EVENTS – PART ONE ......................... 149
LESSON 16: END TIME EVENTS – PART TWO ......................... 158
I'd love to hear from you .................................................................. 165
How to Sponsor a Book Project ...................................................... 166

Other Books by Matthew Robert Payne ................................................. 167
About Matthew Robert Payne ............................................................... 170

The Bible teaches that everyone is born into Satan's kingdom. We therefore need to change direction, or we will end up in Hell. If we commit our life to the Lord Jesus Christ, we will be transferred into the Kingdom of God. The cross of Jesus is the central theme of the Bible. This book on discipleship will help new believers grow in God.

# ACKNOWLEDGEMENTS

I want to thank Father God, the Lord Jesus Christ, and the Holy Spirit for their sacrificial love for mankind. The Holy Spirit is my loving Friend, Comforter, Guide, and Teacher. He gave me the desire to write these lessons, and he also gives me guidance and love for each student. It's wonderful to see someone grow in their knowledge and love for the Lord Jesus Christ and to be eager to know more about his Word.

I particularly want to thank my son, Matthew Robert Payne, for encouraging me to write this book. He will add his thoughts at the end of each chapter. As of the writing of this book in January 2018, he has written and published thirty-four books, available on Amazon. He plans to continue writing as long as the Lord inspires him to do so.

My close friend, Betty Fleming, did the first edit on this book. She is a retired school teacher, but she weekly gives her time to teach English to new Australians at her church.

Without the love and support of my husband, Robert Barry Payne, I wouldn't be the person I am today. He has been my constant protector, my loving soulmate, and my greatest fan throughout the many storms that could have overcome us. We both acknowledge that God is so good. His love is steadfast and sure, and it is a constant anchor for our souls.

I am eternally grateful for the friendship and wise counsel I received from a former neighbor in Sydney, Australia. Betty Jordon displayed Christ-like attributes in everything she did. As a mother herself, she saw my silent call for help and steered me in the right direction.

Don Kemsley, a former pastor at the Coffs Harbour Baptist Church, had a major impact on our family. On behalf of my whole family, I want to thank him for his unique children's stories, which prepared us for every Sunday sermon. Our whole family adored him. He retired years ago, but his incredible love for our Lord Jesus Christ has inspired me to this day.

Once, a close friend of ours and member of the church was about to board a private plane to go on an outback mission. Pastor Don came up to young Matthew and whispered, "You know, Matt, in the future, people are going to send you off on mission trips for our Lord Jesus Christ." Matthew and I believed Don's prophetic words, and even now, after all these years, we know that they will come to pass.

Finally, I want to thank Pastor Brian Eyre at Heartbeat Church Coffs Harbour NSW. Years ago, he called me one day to ask if I would consider teaching new Christians basic Bible truths. I jumped at the chance because I knew that I would really enjoy such an awesome challenge.

# BOOK DEDICATION

This book is dedicated to all my readers and is especially dedicated to those whom the Lord will call to teach others. May they be blessed and encouraged to trust God to teach Scripture in schools, to teach Bible truths to new believers in the privacy of their own home, or to teach at a small study group within their church. Like all Christian endeavors, you will need constant reliance on the Holy Spirit and ongoing practice to accomplish this.

I encourage every seeker of God to keep a permanent bookmark at the index page of their Bible so that they can quickly and easily find a particular passage of Scripture.

To look up a particular Bible verse, find the required book, then find the chapter and finally the verse within the chapter. For example, Romans 10:17 says, "So then faith comes by hearing, and hearing by the word of God." The book of Romans comes immediately after the Book of Acts, which is after the four gospel records of Matthew, Mark, Luke and John. Flip through the pages of Romans until you come to chapter 10 and carefully look down the verses of that chapter until you find verse 17. This particular verse infers that we won't grow in faith if we don't study the Bible because faith comes from hearing (or reading) his instructions to us.

God wants all his family to have a solid knowledge of the basic foundations of the Christian faith. In Matthew 5:6, he promised us, "Blessed are those who hunger and thirst after righteousness for they shall be filled." Reading books about the Bible can never take the place of personally studying it. "All Scripture is given by inspiration of God, and is profitable for doctrine, for reproof, for correction, for instruction in righteousness, that the man of God may be complete thoroughly equipped for every good work" (2 Timothy 3:16-17).

The Bible keeps us focused on God's plan for us—it's like "a lamp to my feet and a light to my path" (Psalm 119:105). Only the Bible reveals God's holy character, and it alone shows us the path to heaven.

If we refuse to believe that we have a natural bias to sin, we will be easily deceived by false teaching. We all need the Spirit of God living in us to keep us on the right path.

# AUTHOR'S HISTORY AND TESTIMONY

After my father died, my mother couldn't bear the thought of living life without him, so she began to pursue New Age teachings on reincarnation. Either my sister or I would go with her to these events. Mom eventually married Max, a Jewish man, and they moved into an apartment together.

When I grew up, I found suitable accommodations in the attic of a two-story boarding house in Sydney. When I initially knocked on the front door, Bob opened it for me as he was boarding there with four other young lads. He said a single lady upstairs wanted to share accommodations." I moved in with her, and soon after, Bob and I began courting.

Bob was a Christian, and I was very attracted to him, but I was cold toward his faith. We married on March 5, 1960. Twelve years later, I became a Christian, and soon after that, Bob recommitted his life to God. Actually, we discovered years later that we shouldn't have married. "Do not be unequally yoked together with unbelievers. For what fellowship has righteousness with lawlessness? And what communion has light with darkness?" (2 Corinthians 6:14).

Mom had approved of our engagement, but I knew she wouldn't be up to organizing a big wedding. I asked for a small reception at a popular restaurant with just her, Max, my sister, and brother-in-law. Mom eventually agreed but insisted on giving us a thousand pounds (about two thousand U.S. dollars at the time) as a wedding gift in place of a formal reception. Bob's parents lived two hours away and couldn't make it to our wedding as they were in the process of moving into a new home.

My mom's gift allowed us to buy a block of land at Canley Vale in the western outskirts of Sydney. The land title deed then enabled us to secure our first home loan. Actually, our bank loan approval came just before the big credit squeeze in the early sixties. For months, we slept in the single bed my dad had made me when I was only two years old. An ironing board served as our dining table for quite some time before my brother-in-law made us a small table, and we felt like royalty.

In 1961, I had a miscarriage. Matthew firmly believes that this baby was a little girl whom the angels have named Talitha. He also believes that little ones in heaven, including aborted babies, are lovingly cared for by heavenly foster mothers.

The following year, we experienced the heartache of a stillborn little girl, six weeks prior to her due date. We named her Karen Michelle. When I was six months pregnant, my doctor had arranged an x-ray for me. Bob later received a letter from him, asking him to come and see him as soon as possible. I knew that something was wrong, and I became so distraught that Bob drove me over to Mom's place, hoping she could console me. We stayed the night, and the next morning, Bob and Max went into the city to see my doctor. They were away for hours, and when I saw Bob carrying a huge bunch of flowers, I wept uncontrollably as he told me that our baby's condition was incompatible to life.

Later, my doctor explained that although my baby's body was perfect, her brain was malformed. He predicted a premature birth, and he was right. I didn't find out until months later, that while I was in hospital, Bob had to arrange a funeral service for our tiny little girl. To this day, he has never talked about it. Even as I write this book, I think how painful it must have been for him to have to arrange a tiny coffin for our little baby girl.

At Mom's insistence, we went on a second honeymoon. Here on the beach for the first time, Bob began to see all little children as absolute miracles of God. While I baked in the sun, he was happily making sand castles for children nearby. A whole new world had opened up to him, for God had done a wonderful miracle in my husband's heart.

As I write this book, I have a vision that when Bob and I are ushered into heaven, we will be greeted by our two grown-up daughters. What a day of rejoicing that will be for all of us!

Praise God, in April 1964, our perfect and precious daughter, Carmen Louise, was born. Bob was absolutely besotted with her. Rodney John was born in 1965, Matthew Robert in 1967, and Antony Maxwell in 1970. Due to health issues, a few days after Antony's birth, my doctor decided to take me back to surgery to prevent further pregnancies.

I will now share my testimony of how I became a born-again believer.

Along our home was a mostly dry creek bed, which led to a storm-water pipe under our front street. This pipe was a magnet to young Rod and Matt. But I knew that if we had a flash flood, they could easily drown. Although I was seven months pregnant with our youngest son, we moved to Toongabbie, another outer suburb in Sydney.

Years later, I realized that this was exactly where God wanted me to be as my new neighbor, Betty Jordan, was a born-again Christian. She soon became my best friend. Betty was a tower of strength, and I loved going to her home because it was so peaceful. She often took Rod or Matt over to her place just to give me a break. Of course, now I realize that God was actually pursuing me through her kind and gentle witness.

As a young child, our oldest son, Rod, had a strange sleeping ritual. In a crawling position, he constantly banged his head on the top end of his crib until he finally fell asleep. We finally discovered that he had been born with glue in his eardrum, which made constant irritating noises in his head. He had an ear operation, but he was still frustrated by head noises. This hearing problem led to a speech problem. The duel frustration of head noises and not being understood made him impatient, angry, and resentful. He couldn't tolerate the slightest inconvenience and thought that head banging helped. Every time he was chastised or frustrated, he banged his head against the wall or on the floor.

Worse still, when he was in second grade, the teacher often had to consult his younger brother to find out what Rod was talking about. He highly resented that! Amazingly, his teacher told us that she had never seen Rod bang his head at school. Finally, he stopped doing it at home. Perhaps Betty had asked God to intervene.

I was so thankful for Betty, but I was very curious and more than a little jealous of her amazing ability to cope with my precious little boy. I really wanted to be like her. One day I said to her, "How do you handle his temper tantrums?"

Without hesitation, she replied, "I let Rodney know from the beginning, that the Lord Jesus Christ is God, and HE is the head of this home, so bad behavior of *any* kind will not be tolerated in God's home." She told Rod to come and see her if he had any problems.

I was astonished, but my silent reaction was, "Bully for you!" But in my heart, I really wanted to be like her. Rod's head-banging finally ceased, but his tantrums at home took a few more years to stop.

One day, Betty invited me to a ladies' convention where I realized for the first time that God wanted to help me simply because he loved me. I discovered that Jesus knew all my concerns and wanted to be my Lord and Savior. I am forever grateful that Betty befriended me. Because of her kindness and prayers, I was converted at that convention in July 1972 when I was thirty-three years old.

It was really a bit freaky because, for years, Mom had told me that, when I was thirty-three, I would begin a very different life. I had silently feared that maybe I would be divorced or some awful tragedy would befall Bob. Never for a moment did I imagine that I would become a brand new person spiritually!

I often told Betty how wonderful my mother was, but one day. I shared with her that Mom regularly saw clairvoyants because she still wanted to contact my dead father. Betty immediately responded, "June, you must understand that your mother is being deceived by evil spirits. She needs to surrender her life to the Lord Jesus Christ. You need to pray for her every single day, June."

She then showed me some verses in her Bible so that I could see for myself that trying to contact the dead was absolutely forbidden by God. From that time on, I made sure that I regularly prayed for Mom's salvation.

Many years later in Coffs Harbour, I was reading Psalm 138, written by King David. Verse 8 said, "The Lord will perfect that which concerns me." I thought, *Mom is my chief concern, and God is going to bring her to perfection*! I was excited and shared this with Bob. Later on, I was reading Isaiah 46:11b. "Indeed I have spoken it; I will also bring it to pass. I have purposed it; I will also do it." I knew in my spirit that God had not forgotten and in his time, he would save my mother.

Nearly every day, I reread my promises, and on March 16, 2008, I heard the Lord audibly say to me, "I will save your Mom." It was the first and only time that I have ever heard the audible voice of the Lord! At church the next day, the pastor asked if the Lord had done something special for anyone in the last week. Without hesitation, I jumped to my feet and announced that God was going to save my mum because he had told me he would. The whole congregation spontaneously clapped their hands as I sat back down.

In God's time, he graciously allowed me to have the awesome privilege of leading my mom to salvation. She had been complaining that she had been in God's waiting room too long, so I gently said to her, "Mom, you are not ready for God to come for you. You need to have God's Holy Spirit living in you. Only then will you be ready to go to heaven."

She instantly filled up with tears and said, "I have never even heard of God's Holy Spirit!"

I explained that God the Holy Spirit is equal to the Father and equal to the Lord Jesus Christ because we have a triune God. The Father lives in heaven. The Son came to earth for a short time to give his life for us, and the Holy Spirit is the one who works in a person's heart and leads them to salvation. God in the form of the Holy Spirit actually longs to live forever in the human spirit of every single person on earth.

I didn't know if she understood my answer, so I briefly shared the gospel with her. She vehemently denied being a sinner, so I explained what sin was in more detail, and she finally admitted, "yes", she was a sinner. She repeated the sinner's prayer after me. Although I was so happy, I was almost crying at that point. She later told me that when she was little, her mother used to read the Bible to her at bedtime every night. She also remembered asking God into her life once after her mother suggested that she should do so. It was such a God moment for both of us, and we just hugged each other.

I bought a large-print, easy-to-read Bible and suggested that she should read about the Lord Jesus Christ and his Holy Spirit in the New Testament BEFORE reading about the Jewish people in the Old Testament.

Later, I made her a *Promises of God* book in large print. I had a plastic folder with twenty inserts in it, so I asked God to give me forty suitable verses for Mom. As I typed up one verse, God would give me another. I thought I was one short, but I later discovered that I had not printed one. I gave this book to Mom, and she was so thrilled.

A few years later, when Mom was ninety-six years old, my sister called to say that she was dying. Bob and I immediately prayed that God would spare her until we made the two-hour trip to Port Macquarie. She clasped my hand when she saw me, but she didn't speak. I was absolutely ecstatic that within the twinkling of an eye, my mother's soul would be taken by an angel into God's presence. Moments before she died, I had just finished singing a well-known chorus to her.

"Turn your eyes upon Jesus,
Look full in His wonderful face,
And the things of earth will go strangely dim,
In the light of His glory and grace."[1]

At her funeral, I was still excited; there was no grief whatsoever! When my pastor asked me if I had something to say, I confidently took the mike and said in absolute triumph, "That coffin only holds the worn-out, empty shell that my mother used for her time on earth. She no longer needs it as she is young and beautiful now, and she is probably dancing in heaven with the angels of God or even with the Lord Jesus Christ himself."

I said a lot more as I was so excited and happy, but one thing I know is that, apart from my wedding day and the birth of my first grandchild, Mom's funeral was one of the most exciting days of my life. The only time I shed a tear was when my sister very quietly and sedately danced a gentle rumba in front of the coffin just before the funeral service began.

She had her back to the congregation, and when she sat down next to me, she was shaking all over. At the time, I didn't know why she had danced, but I knew it must have been extremely important to her. During that gentle rumba, both Bob and I filled up with tears, for we knew that such a public display was totally out of character for my sister.

---

[1] "Turn Your Eyes upon Jesus," Timeless Truths, Accessed January 19, 2018, http://library.timelesstruths.org/music/Turn_Your_Eyes_upon_Jesus.

I found out later that, every time she helped mum out of her recliner-chair, Mom would gently rumba to the bathroom with her. One day, Mom said in all seriousness, "Promise me, darling, that when I am in my coffin, you will play rumba music. Then, if there's any life in me, I will hear the music, and my coffin will start rocking."

My sister replied, "Mom, if you can't rumba at that time, I will rumba for you!" The words were lightly spoken, but when Mom died, my sister knew that she had to honor her promise.

That dance also exposed Satan's lie to me! You see, ever since my salvation and prior to Mom's funeral, I was acutely aware of a spiritual wall between my sister and me. I knew she loved me, but I also knew that Satan wanted to destroy our close relationship. However, that funeral dance absolutely dissolved any form of division between us. God is so good.

My sister hasn't come to the Lord yet, but I am praying that she will when the Holy Spirit gets on her case just like he did for me at that ladies' convention. She is such a compassionate and lovely person. She and her husband have many wonderful friends as they are both so kind and have such welcoming hearts. She can only walk with the use of her walker these days and is mostly confined to her recliner lounge chair. She has been by the bedside of many of her friends on their death bed, but she will not share her beliefs with me. I know one thing for sure: death for a Christian has truly lost its sting.

As I look back on my life, I am so thankful for God's awesome grace during our fifty-seven years of marriage. Yes, we have had our fair share of problems, but God has been good to our family. Bob and I are both grateful to God that I knocked on that boarding-house door in Sydney.

If you feel that you would like to teach basic Bible truths to other believers or seekers of God, go for it! I can promise you, God never calls you to do anything for him without giving you both the desire and the ability to do it. Be sensitive to his leading, and he will direct your steps just like he has always done for me. I love teaching Bible truths to new Christians.

If you have a computer, these lessons can be easily adapted to suit any seeker of God. The Holy Spirit knows where each person is at, so he will lead you in what to say. I discovered that it's best not to give students a lesson summary sheet up front until you discover what God wants you to teach them. If you don't want to write your own lessons as I do, Christian bookstores have a selection of suitable teaching books for you to choose from. You can find additional teaching materials online.

Years ago when I had access to Christian television, I listened to Andrew Wommack's daily teaching sessions while furiously scribbling down notes. I then typed up the message while it was still fresh in my memory. His teaching totally changed my legalistic theology and introduced me to God's incredible grace. Andrew has extremely balanced theology. To me, he is the best speaker I have ever heard in all the forty-five years of being a born-again believer. In fact, much of my teaching is based on his teaching on television.

Once, Andrew's oldest son called his dad, who was driving home from a speaking engagement, to say that his younger brother had died. Andrew turned to his wife and announced, "The first report is NOT the last report!" Five hours later, Andrew prayed for his dead son in the hospital, and immediately the boy sat up, and he suffered absolutely no after effects.

I met Andrew at his conference in Brisbane, Australia, once and asked if my husband and I could have a photo with him. He said, "yes," and another gentleman took the photo. I was overjoyed that such a mighty man of God would so graciously oblige a total stranger.

Andrew's faith in the goodness and grace of God has enabled him to confidently pray over the dead on many occasions, and God answers his prayers of faith! If you are interested in reading his books, a Christian bookstore could order them for you, or you could contact him at PO Box 3333, Colorado Springs, Colorado 80935-3333 or at his email at awommack@aol.com You can also find his books online at Amazon.

Satan has convinced most people that they are good enough to go to heaven. But the Lord Jesus Christ, the Son of God, emphatically said, "I am the way, the truth and the life. No man comes to the Father except through Me" (John 14:6).

People need to know that "good works" will not get them to heaven, for they need to hear and believe the full gospel message. Trust God and tell him that you are willing to do whatever he leads you to do. Remember, God will never ask his own kids to do anything for him without first preparing their hearts and equipping them to be able to do it. *God is a good Dad!*

# **BIBLE LESSONS**

# LESSON 1: GOD HAS ALWAYS BEEN

God is three holy persons in one: Father, Son, and Holy Spirit. They share the same view about everything, but each holy person has a different function. Collectively, these three divine beings make up the Holy Trinity or the Godhead.

God is eternal; he has always been; he had no beginning and will have no end. He knows everything so nothing surprises him. He can also do anything he wants to do.

God is not limited to time or space as he is everywhere at the same time. Our human mind cannot comprehend his divine nature, so we must come to him by faith alone in what the Bible says about him.

- Father God paid the ultimate price for our salvation. He sacrificed his only begotten Son so that we could then choose to live with him in heaven for all eternity or to ignore him completely.

- The obedient Lord Jesus Christ humbled himself and fulfilled his Father's will even to the excruciating pain and humiliation of the cross. He now sits next to Father God in heaven. One day, this unique God-man Jesus Christ will be the supreme judge of the whole world, and he will reign as king on earth for a thousand years!

- God, the Holy Spirit, brings conviction of sin and reveals to us our need of a Savior. If we respond to his call and genuinely repent of our sin, we can ask the Holy Spirit to make his home in our human spirit, for this is his desire for all mankind.

God is *always* good! People wrongly believe that God controls everything, so they blame him for bad outcomes in their lives. But most bad things happen because of our own or someone else's sinful or foolish actions or by demonic powers. James 4:7 says,

"Submit to God. Resist the devil and he will flee from you." If we don't fully submit to God's authority, we can unknowingly open the door to the devil's lies and accusations.

When the Godhead created earth, certain laws were put into motion: the law of gravity, the law of aerodynamics, and so forth. Avalanches and tsunamis happen; volcanoes erupt; rocks fall; lightning strikes; excessive speed kills people and so on. God doesn't cause death through these things. These are laws of nature. Someone you love could have been in the wrong place at the wrong time, and their time on earth was up. Don't blame God for bad things.

I heard Andrew Wommack talk on this subject once. He said something similar to the following: "If something is good, it's God; if it's bad, it's us or others; it's a freak accident, or it's the devil wanting to hurt someone." He implied much the same thing in a book he co-authored with Don Krow called *The Complete Discipleship Evangelism Course: Condensed Version and Workbook*.[2] (I highly recommend this book to all my readers.)

In the same book, Andrew quoted the well-known verse in Romans 8:28. "And we know that all things work together for good to those who love God, to those who are the called according to His purpose." Many people interpret this verse to say that whatever happens in life, God does it, and in some way, works it together for good. Andrew disagrees. He believes that bad things often happen because of human ignorance or carelessness.

Also, be mindful that Ephesians 6:12-18 warns us that there is an ongoing and unseen spiritual battle going on around us all the time. Though the devil has "no legal" authority over a Christian, the Bible says in 1 Peter 5:8, "Be sober, be vigilant; because your adversary the devil walks about like a roaring lion, seeking whom he may devour."

---

[2] Andrew Wommack and Don Krow, *The Complete Discipleship Evangelism Course: Condensed Version and Workbook.* (Europe: Andrew Wommack Ministries, 2007), 53-54.

Romans 8:28 is specifically addressed to "those who love God." This verse is not an open promise to everyone. God is the Creator and Author of everything good, and Satan and his demons rejoice in every form of disaster or evil outcome. (Mind you, the devil delights in using weak believers in the church to hurt their brothers and sisters in the Lord.)

We have each been given a free will, and God wants us to make good choices. Jesus said in John 10:10, "The thief does not come except to steal, and to kill, and to destroy. I have come that they may have life, and that they may have it more abundantly."

God is love, and love rejoices in healthy and strong relationships. A wondrous relationship exists within the three personalities of the Godhead, and God longs to share a love relationship with all people, adults and children everywhere.

We don't know exactly when the angels were created, but they existed in heaven long before the earth was formed. God had given the angels a free will so that they could each choose whether or not to love and worship the Creator.

Lucifer, the most beautiful and talented angel, became increasingly jealous of God's authority and power. He saw himself as equal to God and said, "I will be like the Most High" (Isaiah 14:14). He wanted to receive the same worship that God received. (Actually one-third of the angelic realm bowed down to Lucifer.)

Ultimately, God threw Lucifer and his rebellious followers out of heaven. Today, this former angel of God is mostly referred to as the devil or Satan, and his spiritual followers are known as demons. We learn in Hebrews 1:14 that the remaining two thirds of the angels in heaven are God's supernatural helpers. They are still active in the world today, for they are sent by God to accomplish earthly missions in order to advance the kingdom of God on earth.

I personally believe that at some earlier stage, God must have created a beautiful earth, but when Satan and his demons were cast out of heaven, they made earth a place of desolation.

I say this because everything God creates is good and beautiful, and everything has order. Yet in verse one of Genesis, we read, "The earth was without form and void and darkness was on the face of the deep. And the Spirit of God was hovering over the face of the waters." Perhaps science has an explanation of the words "without form and void." Personally, I would like to know more about the subject.

Now back to the creation account in Genesis. God then made a special light for the day and one for the night. He also placed stars into the night sky. He filled the earth with plant life, animals, insects, birds, fish, and all the sea creatures. Note that all creation at that time came into existence by God's spoken word alone.

We learn in the Gospel of John that the Word of God is the Lord Jesus Christ, "In the beginning was the Word, and the Word was with God, and the Word was God. He was in the beginning with God. All things were made through Him, and without Him nothing was made that was made. In Him was life, and the life was the light of men" (John 1:1-4).

Also in Colossians 1:13-17, we read, "He has delivered us from the power of darkness and conveyed us into the kingdom of the Son of His love, and in whom we have redemption through His blood, the forgiveness of sins. He is the image of the invisible God, the firstborn over all creation. For by Him all things were created that are in heaven and that are on earth, visible and invisible, whether thrones or dominions or principalities or powers. All things were created through Him and for Him. And He is before all things, and in Him all things consist." Jesus is our Creator, Lord, and Redeemer!

The triune God was now ready to create their masterpiece. Note the plurality. "Let us make man in Our image, according to

Our likeness; let them have dominion over the fish of the sea, over the birds of the air, and over the cattle, over all the earth and over every creeping thing that creeps on the earth" (Genesis 1:26).

This new creation would be unique, for it was to be made in God's own image. Rather than just using his voice, God personally fashioned Adam with his own hands. "And the Lord God formed man of the dust of the ground and breathed into his nostrils the breath of life; and man became a living being" (Genesis 2:7). God also provided a complementary life-companion for Adam. He fashioned Eve from one of Adam's ribs.

Like us today, Adam and Eve were given a personal will in their soul area. This special creation was to live forever. God looked forward to sharing his love one day with a huge family who would love him in return. God is love. Love must have an object, a person to love, for love needs relationship. The three personalities of the Godhead have a wondrous relationship, and God wants to share this relationship with his created beings, both male and female.

Unlike the rest of creation, mankind alone has a unique soul and spirit, which will live for eternity. Just where each person's soul and spirit will eternally live depends on whether they respond to God's love demonstrated by the Lord Jesus Christ on the cross over two thousand years ago. If you have not already given your heart to God, then hopefully, the Holy Spirit may use this book to bring you into conviction of your personal sin, and you will come to know the Lord Jesus Christ as your own personal Lord and Savior.

My Bible notes say: "Through Adam and Eve, God intended to manifest His character and authority. Together, they were meant to display God's indisputable power over the works of darkness, and subdue His archenemy, Satan. God wanted His glory to be forever seen throughout the Earth through the combined expression of male and female. For His promise of success was and will always be, based on unity."[3]

God yearns for unity within marriages, within families, within churches, within workplaces, and of course, within countries. But Satan and his demons rejoice in disunity in all forms. Adam and Eve had God's Holy Spirit in their human spirit, for they were meant to live forever, but Satan had a plan which would lead to far-reaching heartache for mankind.

God created man in his own image, for we too are made up of three important parts. We each have a unique human body, which we are responsible to look after. Our body serves as a temporary home for our precious parts to live in, our eternal soul and spirit. Our soul is also made up of three parts, which we will learn about in later lessons.

Our human spirit has been pre-programmed by God for worship! If our spirit doesn't worship the one true Creator God, it will find something else to worship, such as the body beautiful or some kind of false god. Many people focus on striving for wealth or are overly competitive in sports, but a false god can be anything that takes our attention far more than it should.

Having a false belief system, about our Creator-God, gives Satan a perfect opportunity to seriously deceive us in other areas as well. Humans alone have been created in God's image and are meant to glorify God, for he is good, and he wants order and beauty in our lives. Most people are either ignorant of this, or they are much more concerned about temporal things than their inward potential in God and true loveliness.

Free choice is a wonderful gift from God, but it can be extremely dangerous. The Bible teaches, that what we do about the Lord Jesus Christ in this life will determine our afterlife.

---

[3] Jack Hayford, et al., *New Spirit-Filled Life Bible*, (Nashville: Thomas Nelson Bibles, 2013).

Included in this lesson is a condensed gospel message.

**Matthew's Comments**

I am very aware of the Holy Trinity and have come to know each of the three persons of the Godhead in a very real and personal way. Of the three, I have known Jesus the best and spent the most time conversing with him and having him as a friend. A few years ago and later in my life, I started to get to know God as my Father. As I spoke to the Father, I came to find that his voice had more authority in it than that of Jesus when I heard him speak.

It is possible to grow in a great relationship with Jesus, the Father, and the Holy Spirit. The last person of the Trinity I came to know was the Holy Spirit. Some people are led by the Holy Spirit, by thoughts that he gives them that they are not aware of. That is one way to be led by the Holy Spirit, but a more personal and effective way to be led by the Holy Spirit is to hear his voice speak to your thoughts, where you actually know that he is speaking.

He can tell you to take your umbrella because while you are out that day it will rain.

That is one way my life was affected by the Holy Spirit. I once asked him if he could warn me any day that it was going to rain and when I would get wet if I did not take an umbrella. He has been faithful to honor that request, and he has always told me. Some days, it has rained when I was out, and I have been led to doubt that he answered my request because he didn't tell me to take an umbrella, and yet when it comes time to go home, it turns out that the sky was clear with no rain.

Like I have said, I have come to know the Father in the past few years. I have started to record conversations with him that I made into books for people to read and learn from. They can be bought and read by you when you click on the links below.

*Conversations with God: Book 1*
*Conversations with God: Book 2*
*Conversations with God: Book 3*

I have to agree with the well-known thoughts of my mother that say we are made up of a spirit, soul, and body. I am very aware of my spirit, that part of me that is pure, clean, and holy. I am aware that my soul (my mind, will, and emotions) is corrupted by sin and loves to lead me into doing things that are not helpful. I also know that when I fast and starve my body of food or sleep, my spiritual anointing increases for a time. My understanding of these three parts of us that make us up is not theory but a factual part of my life.

I also need to comment on free will and mankind. Many people say that God is in control of everything, and many Christians believe that this is true; however, that is not the case. Many people do very cruel and evil things by their own choice and their free will that God has given them, and as a result, people suffer. This suffering experienced by people at the hands of others is not in God's control and is certainly not God's will. But God has given all men free will, and so man can choose to do good or to do evil, and God does not leave heaven every time that someone decides to do bad things. It is important for the readers to realize this even if you have to do more reading on this subject. When you believe that God is in control of everything, you can become very upset at God.

# LESSON 2: PARADISE LOST AND CONDENSED GOSPEL MESSAGE

Adam and Eve were created as innocent, and for a time, they enjoyed wonderful fellowship with God. One day, God tested Adam's loyalty by telling him in Genesis 2:17 not to eat from a particular tree, or he would die. That tree was called the "tree of the knowledge of good and evil," and the other was called the "tree of life."

Satan saw Adam and Eve as useful tools to hurt God. He cunningly disguised himself as a serpent, and in Genesis 3:1-6, he questioned Eve about God's goodness. She had childlike innocence with no understanding that Satan wanted to destroy her relationship with God. Satan still hates God, and he delights to use the mouth or the actions of others to stir up trouble, but we can't blame Satan for everything bad in life.

First Eve, then Adam, made a bad choice, and today, we too often become victims of our own bad choices in life. Eve was genuinely deceived by the serpent, but Adam was responsible to God to protect her. He should have stopped her from eating the forbidden fruit, but instead, he foolishly ate from the tree himself. He ignored God's instructions, and instead of using his authority to challenge the serpent, he yielded to his own bodily appetite.

From that time on, original sin is only ever spoken of as Adam's sin, for in the sight of God, he was held accountable for his wife's well-being. This one decision by Adam forever polluted the human gene pool as everyone born since that time has been born spiritually dead and therefore separated from God. In other words, everyone at some stage in their life must be spiritually reborn in order to be reconciled back to God.

The devil, of course, does his best to keep people ignorant of this biblical reality.

Genesis 3 doesn't say that Adam and Eve instantly fell down dead at the base of the tree. No, this is because they both died spiritually not physically. At that point, God the Holy Spirit left their human spirit because they had disobeyed God. Previously, the Holy Spirit had lived within their inner spirit.

The human spirit longs to worship, and if it doesn't worship the one true God, it will find someone or something else to worship. Thankfully, God, at great personal cost, made a way that we can be spiritually reconciled back to him. At some stage in life, everyone needs to personally respond to God's love demonstrated on the cross of Jesus Christ.

Adam and Eve had eaten from the tree of the knowledge of good and evil, but if they then ate from the tree of life, all future generations would have been separated from God forever. God had to expel them from paradise (the Garden of Eden), and he placed angel guards to stop them from returning. They went on to populate the earth, but their sin nature has been passed on to every generation since that time. Adam and Eve physically died hundreds of years later, for back then, life expectancy was vastly longer than today.

Ever since that one act of disobedience, everyone at birth is spiritually separated from God. But God in his grace intervenes in the case of a small child's death. Babies and toddlers are seen as innocent until they come to a proper age of knowing right from wrong.

The really tragic outcome of Adam's sin was that it eventually led to the crucifixion of our Lord Jesus Christ. What parent today could, in love, agree to the sacrifice of their only child for someone else? Thankfully, both Father God and his Son's love for mankind are far deeper and more sacrificial than our love for others.

1 Corinthians 15:22 says, "For as in Adam all die, even so in Christ all shall be made alive." Therefore, although we are born spiritually dead, we can, by God's grace, be made alive in Christ.

If we do make that choice, our human spirit will be infused with God's Holy Spirit. This alone results in a person being spiritually born again!

Being born spiritually dead makes us cold toward the gospel message. Also, no matter how good we try to live, we will never in our own strength be able to reach the holy standard of God. That is why our Lord Jesus Christ stressed the importance of being born again. He told a highly respected Jewish religious leader, "Most assuredly, I say to you, unless one is born again, he cannot see the kingdom of God" (John 3:3).

Our human spirit must be infused with God's Holy Spirit if we want to enjoy heaven one day. Otherwise, we will be separated from God forever in a place we don't want to be.

If you, my reader, have not yet been re-born spiritually by the power of God's Holy Spirit, I suggest that you ask the Lord to soften your heart so that you will be open to the gospel message. None of us know how long our days on earth will be. Realize that no matter how good we try to be, the fact remains that we are all sinners at birth and are on the road to hell. Satan does his best to prevent people from knowing their eternal destiny.

Most people consider themselves to be "good" and are highly offended if told that they need salvation. Unbelievers tend to think that shortcomings like inner pride, lying, gossiping, and even cheating at times is okay. They think that only really "bad" people will miss out on heaven. But in God's sight, this is wrong theology. The truth is that any wrongdoing or wrong thinking is sin, and left to our own understanding, no one would ever be saved!

Only God the Holy Spirit can convict us of sin, and he often uses our conscience to tell us, but often we suppress that quiet inner voice.

The news that we are all sinners is hard to accept, but hearing that the Lord Jesus Christ took the punishment for all sin upon himself is definitely good news. I am so thankful that my godly neighbour really loved me. She cared enough for me and my children to share the good news that the Son of God left heaven to die for all mankind. Our part is to personally respond to God's grace demonstrated on the cross.

Satan lies about God's goodness, and he drops these lies into our mind. In ignorance, we often blame God for bad things when it's not God but Satan who delights to hurt us. Because God knows the future, he knew even in the Garden of Eden that Satan would win the first round. But God had a painful and personal "rescue plan" in mind for all humanity.

Satan loves to see people angry, sick, hurt, poor, fearful, and suffering. He wants to cheat us out of all the good things in life and to keep us from ever knowing the extravagant love of God. Instead of being angry with each other, we need to understand that Satan is always our real enemy. The enemy is not other people, and it certainly isn't God. The devil delights in evil.

God had a rescue mission in mind long before he created Adam and Eve because God knows the future; he is never surprised!

God is love, but he is fair and just as well because his nature is holy! Holiness demands that sin is punished not simply overlooked. His divine nature always wants to love and forgive us. Father God, Lord Jesus Christ, and the Holy Spirit together made a way that all people could live in heaven for all eternity, but it is conditional!

We each need to truly confess to him that we are sinners by nature, and thank the Lord Jesus Christ for dying on the cross for us. Finally, we need to ask God the Holy Spirit to live in our human spirit forever. All this can be summed up with the words, "being born again."

Over two thousand years ago, God the Holy Spirit performed a miraculous conception inside the physical womb of a righteous Jewish virgin named Mary. Jesus Christ, though he was God, was born fully human, yet he was filled with the Holy Spirit from birth.

Jesus as a man was like any born-again believer except he alone was sinless! Jesus was on earth for thirty-three years. He devoted his whole life to pleasing Father God, knowing that, one day, he would suffer an agonizing death on a Roman cross for the collective sin of mankind.

Jesus warned his disciples that he would be soon leaving them and said, "If you love Me, keep My commandments. And I will pray the Father, and He will give you another Helper, that He may abide with you forever" (John 14:15-16). The spiritual helper of every Christian is God the Holy Spirit. He enters the inner soul of every believer the moment they come to salvation.

As a Jew, Jesus attended the Jewish synagogue and kept the Jewish holy days. The two most important Jewish festival days were and still are the Feast of Passover and the Day of Atonement. Jesus knew his rescue mission would be almost over as it was the time of Passover. He knew that soon, he would be crucified and be with his Father in heaven again.

As a believer today, we have total assurance that we have been redeemed by the blood of the Lamb. (See Peter 1:19.) The unique Lamb of God, our Lord Jesus Christ, actually did away with the need for Jewish sacrificial priesthood. Jesus suffered the penalty of sin for all mankind. People need to personally acknowledge this truth and accept him as the Lord and Saviour of their life.

Out of pride or ignorance, the majority of people have not responded to God's amazing love. Also today, the majority of Old Testament Jewish believers have not recognized that Jesus on the cross has once and forever fully satisfied the requirements of the Old Testament law.

In the Old Testament, on the tenth day of the Jewish month of Abib (March/April on our calendar), every Jewish family had to select for themselves a perfect one-year-old male lamb. It was to be brought into the family home and treated like a pet for a short time. Then, it was ceremoniously killed as the family's sacrificial offering to God so that their sin could be forgiven for another year.

Back then, God was trying to teach the Jewish people, that only the blood of an innocent lamb could atone for personal sin. But nearly two thousand years later, Jesus, the perfect Lamb of God, was arrested and savagely beaten by the Roman soldiers. He was brutally hung on a cross outside of the city to be crucified. On either side of him were two criminals. For six agonizing hours, the Son of God hung on that torturous cross.

The Roman custom was to eventually break the legs of those on the cross so that they couldn't push down on their feet to lift themselves up and breathe out. But Jesus needed to fulfil the prophetic word in Psalm 34:20 that says, "He guards all his bones, not one of them is broken." At 3:00 p.m., Jesus proclaimed, "It is finished!" He then surrendered his spirit up to his Father. Later in the afternoon when the soldiers came to break his legs, they discovered that he was already dead. Not a bone had been broken for he surrendered his life to God willingly and just died.

At that particular time, Jesus had been acutely aware that the high priest in the temple was conducting the annual Passover service, and just as he surrendered his life to God, a perfect, young, male lamb was being ceremoniously slaughtered for the atonement of the people's sin.

Most Jewish people deny that Christ Jesus on the cross was the perfect Passover Lamb of God.

Christians worldwide know that man didn't take the life of Jesus. The Son of God gave his life willingly, and everything went according to plan on that gruesome crucifixion day. Since that time, Gentiles—that is, all non-Jewish people—celebrate Good

Friday and have a special Easter Service in the church of their choice.

Even if people don't regularly attend church, many of them attend services either on Good Friday or on Resurrection Sunday. People instinctively know that Easter is important even though they might not be born-again believers. Even Easter buns have a cross on top of them.

At the Jewish temple, at the very moment that Jesus laid down his life, another significant event occurred. We read these words in Matthew 27:51-54, "Then behold, the veil of the temple was torn in two from top to bottom; and the earth quaked, and the rocks were split, and the graves were opened; and many bodies of the saints who had fallen asleep were raised; and coming out of the graves after His resurrection, they went into the holy city and appeared to many. So when the centurion and those with him, who were guarding Jesus, saw the earthquake and the things that had happened, they feared greatly, saying, 'Truly this was the Son of God!'"

My Bible notes say, "The veil was a thick curtain between the Holy Place and the Holy of Holies (see Hebrews 6:19, 10:3, and 10:20.) It was torn in two from the top to bottom, indicating that this was not an act of man, but of God."[4]

Jesus's death and resurrection opened the way for the very presence of God to enter a believer's spirit. Actually, the resurrection of Jesus puts an end to the Old Testament sacrificial system.

Today, all born-again believers of the finished work of Christ on the cross belong to the New Testament priesthood of God. 1 Peter 2:9 says, "But you are a chosen generation, a royal priesthood, a holy nation, His own special people; that you may

---

[4] Hayford, *The New Spirit-Filled Life Bible*.

proclaim the praises of Him who called you out of darkness into His marvelous light."

Jesus was crucified on a Friday and rose from the dead early on Sunday morning! This is why Christians meet for worship on a Sunday whereas the Jewish holy day is a Saturday. But some Messianic Jews worship Jesus as Lord of their life, and they meet in various places around the world even today.

Mary Magdalene, Peter, and John went to the tomb early Sunday morning, and they were astonished that the heavy stone had been rolled away. They went inside the tomb and saw that the cloth that had been around the head of Jesus and was not lying with the linen cloths but folded in a place by itself. They were confused but soon discovered that Jesus had miraculously risen from the dead even though the tomb had earlier been sealed and heavily secured by the Roman guards.

His "resurrected" body was later seen by Mary Magdalene, Joanna, Mary mother of James, and the two men on the Emmaus Road. His eleven remaining disciples had fellowship with their risen Lord. "He also presented Himself alive after His suffering by many infallible proofs, being seen by them during forty days and speaking of the things pertaining to the kingdom of God." (See Acts 1:3.)

Father God wants us all to come to him through the Lord Jesus Christ, for there is no other way that people can be saved from the penalty of inherited and personal sin. Jesus is the only path to heaven (John 14:6).

Yes, the Saviour of the whole world paid the ultimate price for the forgiveness of sin, but many people out of pride or ignorance refuse to respond to his offer. Why? I believe that people compare themselves to others instead of comparing themselves to the goodness of God.

God has the final say as to who will live with him in heaven for all eternity. Those who ask Jesus to come into their heart must also be willing to trust him totally. Trying to be good enough for heaven in our own strength is absolutely impossible to do.

No one can say they have never lied, have never been proud or gossiped about other people. We do these things because we have all inherited a sin nature from Adam. But if we don't receive spiritual re-birth from Jesus before we die, we will be separated from God forever in hell. That's a horrible thought, but it is biblical.

Jesus said to his disciples, "Do not fear those who kill the body but cannot kill the soul. But rather fear Him who is able to destroy both soul and body in hell" (Matthew 10:28). Jesus also said, "I am He who lives, and was dead, and behold, I am alive forevermore. Amen. And I have the keys of Hades and of Death." Revelation 1:18. (Hades is another name for hell.)

- Adam was created sinless. He chose to disobey. Sin became part of the human gene pool.
- For someone to die as a perfect sacrifice for the world, they themselves must be sinless.
- Sin polluted the whole world. God is the only one who is sinless.
- The God-man Jesus Christ took the consequences of the world's sin upon his own body.
- God is still "the boss" of the whole world, and Jesus said that he was the only way to God in John 14:6. Jesus Christ was the only sinless man because he IS God!

**Matthew's Comments**
I was saved when I was eight and was told that I could have a friend in my life that would never leave me. I don't remember being called a sinner and being told I was being saved from sin. As a child, I easily believed in Jesus. I can understand it when older people have an issue with calling themselves a sinner. It must be

hard to accept that they need a Saviour and even harder to come under the lordship of Jesus.

When Adam and Eve first ate of the tree of the knowledge of good and evil, this set in motion so many harmful things in the world. Every person since has been born with a sin nature. When you are born again, you learn to walk with the Holy Spirit in unison. You allow your sin nature to be co-crucified with Christ so that you can break free of the cycle of sin.

I am forever thankful for the life of Christ and for being able to read testimonies of his life and see the example he set for me. I am thankful for his death on the cross that made it possible for me to be forgiven so that I could receive the Holy Spirit into my life. The older I get, the more thankful I become for the life of Jesus and how he has positively affected my life. It helps also that I have a relationship with Jesus and the Holy Spirit and can not only talk to them but be led each day by them in what they want me to do and say.

**A CONDENSED GOSPEL MESSAGE**
The Godhead or the Trinity is God the Father, God the Son, and God the Holy Spirit. All three took part in creation, and they have identical thoughts and power. God wanted someone to pour his great love upon, so for his pleasure, he created a family of his own on earth.

Adam and Eve failed the test of obedience, so God's Holy Spirit left them. Since then, everyone is born with Adam's sin nature, and they need to be spiritually re-born because sin and God cannot co-exist together! The Bible teaches in Romans 3:10 that without God, no human is truly good. We all need the Holy Spirit to come and live in our human spirit.

God's sin solution was for Father God to send his own Son to earth to take upon himself the punishment for all mankind's collective sin—past, present, and future.

Only two men have ever been born sinless. One was Adam, but he soon chose to sin. The other was Jesus Christ, who chose NOT to sin. Twice, Jesus displayed righteous anger, but he never sinned. His work on earth was to glorify his Father in heaven, so he only ever did what his Father told him to do. Like a born-again believer, Jesus had the Holy Spirit of God, guiding him and helping him in his earthly mission.

Jesus on earth was fully God and fully man, both at the same time. As a man, he was given a free will, so he could have sinned if he had chosen to. But Jesus never lost sight of His mission to glorify his Father at all times. He knew that by remaining sinless, he was the only one who could die for someone else's sin. Everyone else dies for their own sin! The Bible calls Jesus "the second Adam." His perfect love for his Father and his genuine love for humanity gave him the strength to surrender to the torture of the Cross.

The sacrifice of Jesus on the cross made a way for those who choose to believe on him and to receive by faith the forgiveness of sin. We need to place our faith in Father God's sin solution alone as there is no other way to enter heaven. We must personally accept Jesus as our own Lord and Savior, for we can't save ourselves no matter how good we try to be because we have an inbuilt sin-bias. We need the indwelling Holy Spirit to help us please God.

Admit to God that you are a sinner who needs forgiveness and then invite the Lord Jesus Christ into your heart. Immediately after you do this, you are spiritually re-born, and you have instantly received the following:

- God gave you his Holy Spirit so that you could live a God-pleasing life for all eternity.
- God forgave your sin so that you are no longer separated from him.
- God gave you a royal inheritance by adopting you into his own royal family.

At the moment of death, Jesus will take you to heaven to live there for all eternity. "For God so loved the world that He gave His only begotten Son that whoever believes in Him will not perish but have everlasting life" (John 3:16).

**Matthew's Comments**

I can imagine that it might be hard for people to come to the realization that they need to be saved and born again through Christ Jesus. We live in a world that gives us hours and hours of television programming but little actual truth in life and especially not the message of salvation.

The life and death of Jesus was no easy feat. It was not easy for Jesus to do. Even Jesus, with all his power and righteousness, struggled to follow through with his intended death on the cross. He cried out in the garden for his Father to take the cup of suffering from him before he was taken by the guards.

We all have Jesus as our model. The righteous way might not always be the easiest path for us, but we can be sure that God and his angels will be with us as we make the tough choices and walk righteously.

# LESSON 3: PART 1 – SPIRIT, SOUL, AND BODY

"May the God of peace Himself sanctify you completely; and may your whole spirit, soul, and body be preserved blameless at the coming of our Lord Jesus Christ" (1 Thessalonians 5:23). Christians generally understand that the word sanctify means to be set apart for God's glory and for his holy purposes.

Just as God is a three-part person, we too have three unique parts: spirit, soul, and body. To God, our spirit is the most important part, and to him, our body is the least important part. He always sees us as eternal and spiritual beings, for we will all live for eternity either with God in heaven or with the devil in hell, depending on who we choose to serve on earth.

I highly suggest that you read the book, *Spirit, Soul and Body* by Andrew Wommack, and you will learn far more about this topic than what can be explained in this brief lesson. Understanding what we have in Christ will free us from accepting the devil's lies about us because we cannot determine the true state of our soul by our intellect or emotions. Instead, we must only believe what the Bible says about us.

While our body is only temporary and is clearly seen, our soul and spirit are eternal and unseen. In his book, Andrew has a simple diagram representing our soul. He has drawn a large circle, and within this circle, he has divided it into another two inner circles. These three divisions are:

1. The outer circle represents our physical body that will die one day and return to dust.
2. The middle circle represents our eternal soul, i.e. our will, intellect, and emotions.
3. The inner circle represents our spirit, which needs to be born-again. This term means that our human spirit is to be

infused with God's Holy Spirit so that we can live forever with God in heaven after our physical death.

Our personal will in our soul is our decision maker. As unbelievers, our will was focused on our fleshly thoughts and emotions and about what we believed was best for us.

But when we surrender our life to the lordship of Jesus Christ, our will needs to come into line with God's choice for us. This means our thoughts and emotions need to come into line as well. But God does not force his will onto anyone.

Our soul is what makes us unique from anyone else. Our soul gives us our personality. We look at a person and see their body. But when we observe their actions and hear their speech, we see their soul. For example, identical twins might look exactly alike, but their souls are uniquely different because they each have a personal will with personal thoughts and emotions.

We are constantly in touch with our body and our soul as they let us know when things are not quite right. But our inner spirit cannot be accessed by our natural thoughts and emotions. Only by the Spirit of God can we understand the state of our inner soul. Jesus said to a religious man, "Most assuredly, I say to you, unless one is born again, he cannot see the kingdom of God" (John 3:3).

NOTE: When you give your heart to Jesus, only your spirit is born again.

After salvation and as we grow in the Lord, God's Holy Spirit in our human spirit will gradually retrain our will, our mind, and our emotions to line up with God's will for us. Being born again happens just once, but changing lifetime habits is an ongoing process.

Again, as Jesus said in John 3:3, we must be born again to see the kingdom of God. A person is reborn spiritually the instant they invite Jesus Christ to come into their life as their personal Lord and

Saviour. At that moment, their human spirit is infused with God's Holy Spirit, and they experience a spiritual rebirth. Understanding this topic will unlock all the Kingdom blessings we have in Christ.

We can only discover what our born-again spirit in our inner soul is like by reading the Bible. We can't do this by our intellect, by our emotions, or by looking in the mirror. We must see God's Word as our spiritual mirror, and we must believe that what it says about us is true.

God says in 2 Corinthians 5:17, "Therefore, if anyone is in Christ, he is a new creation; old things have passed away; behold, all things have become new." This verse is talking about the inner spirit part of our soul. Here, every believer is a brand-new creation.

The apostle James warns us not to project a false image of ourselves to others. He said in James 1:22-24, "Be doers of the word, and not hearers only, deceiving yourselves. For if anyone is a hearer of the word and not a doer, he is like a man observing his natural face in a mirror; for he observes himself, goes away, and immediately forgets what kind of man he was."

A healthy soul focuses on God and what is precious to him, but Satan will constantly put up road blocks to prevent us from pleasing God. Therefore, our personal will within our soul continually has to make important decisions: whether to do what we think is right or to follow the inner promptings of God in our born-again spirit.

As the official keeper of our soul, we need to continually fortify ourselves by reading and believing God's Word. This is very important because an ongoing spiritual battle between the Kingdom of God and Satan's kingdom rages in our soul.

<u>THE KINGDOM OF GOD:</u> This kingdom is "righteousness and peace and joy in the Holy Spirit" (Romans 14:17).

This kingdom consists of the Father, Jesus Christ, and the Holy Spirit, angels of God, and every Christian in heaven and on earth.

Temple worship during the time of the Old Testament consisted of various offerings of grains, birds or other animals. The Jews presented their offering to the priest in order to atone for their personal sins.

But after the resurrection of our Lord, many of the Jewish people became Christians and no longer worshipped God according to Jewish law. The apostle Paul and the early Christians knew that the Lord Jesus Christ on the cross and his supernatural resurrection was positive proof that he was God's perfect Lamb of God, sacrificed once and forever for the collective sin of mankind. Today, believers focus on the goodness of Father God and the obedience of the Lord Jesus Christ.

We are saved not by the works we have done, but by the grace of God. (See Titus 3:5-7.) A common Christian definition of God's grace is: "The free unmerited favor of God toward people who don't deserve it."

SATAN'S KINGDOM: This kingdom brings counterfeit religions, guilt, confusion, doubt, fear, pride, rebellion, destruction, despair, sickness, poverty, and every kind of evil. The kingdom consists of Satan and his demons and all unbelievers since Adam. This kingdom wants to destroy all creation and all people everywhere, including their relationships, their health, their prosperity, and their dreams. The prime aim is to keep people from believing the gospel.

Because of Adam's sin, we are all born into Satan's kingdom, and only Jesus has the authority to transfer us into God's Kingdom. Jesus wants to set people free from Satan's power and control.

In the physical world, we can apply for a dual passport and enjoy dual citizenship, but there is no such thing in the unseen spiritual world. Our soul either belongs to the Kingdom of God or to the kingdom of Satan. Jesus clearly stated, "He who is not with Me is against Me" (Matthew 12:30). If we don't surrender ourselves to Jesus in this life, then God forever sees us as opposed to him.

Therefore, what we do about Jesus Christ will determine our afterlife. Everyone starts off in Satan's kingdom, but if we choose to commit our life to Jesus, we will live forever in God's Kingdom. This truth is the prime reason this book has been written. We each need to make the right choice.

Most unbelievers are either ignorant or confused about the two spiritual kingdoms. They form their opinions only by what they see, hear, touch, taste, or smell in the visible world around them. But the unseen world influences our thoughts and behavior far more than our five senses!

People must learn to be able to distinguish between what comes from God and what comes from Satan. All believers are meant to be God's walking-and-talking light to influence others to become part of God's Kingdom just like my friend Betty Jordon in Sydney who influenced me to give my heart to Jesus.

Most unbelievers embrace heaven but vehemently scoff at a place called hell. Often, if an unbeliever goes to church, they attend out of the religious duty expected from a good, moral person.

But many people genuinely seek God and go to church because God's Holy Spirit is working in their lives and drawing them to the Lord Jesus Christ.

We only have one life on earth because the Bible teaches judgment and resurrection, not reincarnation. However, it suits Satan's purposes for people to believe in reincarnation for he knows "that path" is one of the many popular paths that lead to Hell.

Jesus said in Matthew 7:13-14, "Enter by the narrow way; for wide is the gate and broad is the way that leads to destruction, and there are many who go in by it. Because narrow is the gate and difficult is the way which leads to life, and there are few who find it."

If we want to live in heaven with God for all eternity, then we need to be spiritually reborn by receiving God's Holy Spirit into our lives. Regardless of any so-called goodness in us, we will not be qualified to enter heaven if we do not have God's Holy Spirit residing in our spirits.

Before salvation, our personal identity or self-worth was based on our achievements or the approval of others. These gave us a warm feeling of satisfaction and peace. If we performed well, we felt good about ourselves. If we failed, we became more driven in our desire to succeed in life. Rejection of any kind left us with a poor self-image.

We also needed to keep up our appearance to others because we valued or judged ourselves and other people by outward appearance. This is the world's way. We felt our outer appearance to others was what actually mattered to them. Therefore, if we looked good on the outside, we felt good on the inside.

In contrast, God sees our body as temporary. He is, however, very interested in our eternal spirit and soul.

God really wants us to join him in heaven one day, but we need to have a genuine relationship with his Son here on earth before we die. Before salvation, our life was continually self-focused, and God hardly came into our thinking. We might have said that we believed in God, but we lived our day-to-day lives independent of him.

We were prideful and easily took offense at the actions of others. We struggled to forgive others and held grudges against them. This was normal because we were actually influenced by

Satan who is the god of this world. (See 2 Corinthians 4:4) We might have denied the devil's existence, but he actually ruled our soul even though we thought we were good people. We might have believed that God existed, but we were not conscious of a sin barrier separating us from him.

If something felt good or if all our friends were involved in certain activities, we joined them. We didn't plan to hurt others, but it was our life, and we pleased ourselves. We just wanted to be happy. We certainly didn't want to be seen as nerds or party poopers or worse still, a religious freak, but how others saw us was a high priority. Compared to others, we genuinely thought we were good.

The main problem that all unbelievers have is that they tend to measure themselves against others instead of measuring themselves against the standard of Jesus Christ. Worse still, some of our church-going friends might seem to do the same thing.

Praise God, he sees our new identity in Christ as totally opposite to that of our old nature. Although we might struggle with resisting old thought patterns that belonged to our old nature on a day-to-day basis, *God now sees us as already perfect!* When He looks at believers, he delights in their born-again spirit in their soul, and in his sight, *they are already perfect!*

God wants us to live with our hope and faith firmly established in the person and the work of Jesus Christ. In spirit, every born-again Christian is identical with God's Son, our Lord Jesus Christ. Therefore, allow the Holy Spirit to work with us in training our thoughts, our emotions, and our actions to conform to God's will for us.

The process of sanctification is a lifetime work of us co-operating with God's Holy Spirit in us. God has set us apart for his holy purposes, just like the vessels used by the priests in the Jewish temple were sanctified or set apart for God's holy purposes.

**Matthew's Comments:**
Most people might struggle with the idea that their soul is distinct from their spirit. One way that I can tell that my mind is an enemy of my spirit is when I attempt to have two-way conversations with Jesus. When I try and start a conversation, I find that it is sometimes very difficult to still my mind from thinking. Whenever I try to hear from Jesus and have a conversation in my mind, my carnal mind suddenly begins to think all kinds of distracting thoughts.

My spirit wants to talk to Jesus. I have settled myself and decided to speak with Jesus, and as soon as I start to speak and hear Jesus speak back to me in my mind, my natural mind takes off and starts to think all sorts of thoughts with its own will. In that instance, I can plainly see that my mind (soul) and my spirit are two different parts of me. You can read more about how to speak to God in two-way conversations in my book, _How to Hear God's Voice: Keys to Conversational Two-Way Prayer_.

From time to time, I have gone on a fast where I missed two to three meals a day. When you subject your body to a fast, you become very aware at just how demanding your body is and how it dulls your spiritual sensitivity. Fasting can therefore be used to increase your spirit's ability to tune into God.

Another way I sometimes connect more fully with God is to go without sleep. Depriving the body of needed sleep, which is a type of fast, can also increase your spiritual awareness and put you into another dimension spiritually.

So from my examples, my soul becomes active and fights my spirit when I try to speak to Jesus. When I fast, my spirit becomes more active as I starve my body. When I fast sleep, my spirit becomes more active as I deprive my body of sleep. You can see that we are made up of spirit, soul, and body, and these three parts are intertwined, affecting the other parts of us, depending on our intent, how we go about things, and even on our level of spiritual maturity.

The enemy, Satan, would like you to think that he does not exist. If he can't convince you of that fact, he will attempt to make you ineffective as a Christian. But you can do damage to the kingdom of darkness through informative books, seasoned teachers, and the application of helpful Christian knowledge in your personal life.

# LESSON 4: PART 2 - SPIRIT, SOUL, AND BODY

As believers in the Lord Jesus Christ, we have the blessed assurance that God the Holy Spirit who began a good work in us at salvation will complete his work (Philippians 1:6). Yet, though we are one in Christ, every human soul is unique for we all have different personalities, backgrounds, opportunities, abilities and desires.

While God longs to intervene in the soul health of everyone, he patiently bides his time and gently waits until he knows a person will be open to him. Unbelievers all over the world desperately need to repent of their sin so that their soul can be cleansed. "The Lord is not slack concerning His promise, as some count slackness, but is longsuffering toward us, not willing that any should perish but that all should come to repentance" (2 Peter 3:9).

"Who (God) desires all men to be saved and to come to the knowledge of the truth. For there is one God and one Mediator between God and men, the Man Christ Jesus, who gave Himself a ransom for all, to be testified in due time" (1 Timothy 2:4-6).

The sacrifice of his only Son proved once and for all that Father God wants the whole world to personally accept his offer of salvation. Yet most people remain preoccupied with their careers or with the appearance of their body and temporary pleasures. I sometimes wonder if, in God's eyes, this is like a very young child's preoccupation with gift-wrapping paper instead of the actual gift.

To know God, our human spirit must be infused with God's Holy Spirit. The Bible calls this being born again. Jesus said in John 3:5, "Most assuredly, I say to you, unless one is born of water and the Spirit, he cannot enter the kingdom of God." When spiritual birth takes place, we no longer belong to Satan's kingdom but become members of God's Kingdom.

The new birth only takes place in the spirit part of our soul. Slowly over time, as we read and obey God's Word, our emotions, thoughts, and actions will line up more with God's will for us. We will be able to emotionally and to mindfully think things through before we take action. But our personal will in our soul ultimately determines our actions about everything.

Our decision-making ability is so important that our will ultimately leads us to eternal spiritual life or eternal spiritual death. But we don't have to actually feel something for it to be real in our spirit because we can't feel the spirit part of us. Therefore, whether we feel loved or not, we need to rest in the fact that God deeply loves all of us.

Be mindful that our born-again spirit desires to operate by faith in what God says whereas the natural human spirit might fight against God's Word. God told the apostle John in John 6:63, "It is the Spirit who gives life; the flesh profits nothing. The words that I speak to you are spirit, and they are life." The term flesh in this verse refers to both our eternal soul and our temporary body. These are both constantly speaking to us, but they can easily deceive us.

Once again, our will ultimately determines our actions. We need to continually reprogram our minds to what God's Word says because our minds play a huge part in our decision making within our soul. By faith in God's goodness, we are to believe what he says about us in the Bible. We must know that unbelievers as well as Satan or his demons can speak lies to our soul, causing it to be deceived or manipulated. Untruths or outright lies could then influence our free-will actions.

God's Holy Spirit will little by little illuminate God's Word to us in order to transform our soul, thus bringing biblical understanding to us. The more we read God's Word, the healthier our soul will become and the less likely it is that we will be deceived. It is no wonder that Satan does all he can to prevent us from reading the Bible.

Although we can experience God's love, we must also understand it. If we don't fully understand something, Satan will steal truth from us. "When anyone hears the word of the kingdom, and does not understand it, then, the wicked one comes and snatches away what was sown in his heart" (Matthew 13:19a). Ask the Holy Spirit or your pastor to explain what you don't understand.

The apostle Paul said in 1 Corinthians 6:17, "He that is joined to the Lord is one spirit with him." This verse tells us that our born-again spirit is one with Jesus, so God will never leave us or forsake us. Instead, he will continue to guide and teach us.

We look in the mirror to see our bodies, but bear in mind that others can see our souls just by our attitudes, speech, and actions. To God, however, one-third of every believer *is already perfect*: our born-again spirit in our soul. For this reason we read in 1 John 4:17 that "Love has been perfected among us in this: that we may have boldness in the day of judgment; because as He is, so are we in this world." We should memorize this verse so that we can use it to fight Satan's lies and accusations about us.

We must believe what God has told us in his Word, for it's impossible to judge our born-again spirit by how we feel. Jesus said in John 4:24, "God is Spirit, and those who worship Him must worship Him in spirit and in truth." Therefore, we see that feelings can lead us astray.

As we learn more about God and put into practice what he tells us, the other areas of our soul will slowly change, but it's a life-long process. The Bible calls this process sanctification, which means being set apart, moment by moment, for God's holy purposes.

I have listed some changes below that have already happened in a born-again life.

- Your sin nature died, and you received the nature of Christ (Romans 8:1-2, Galatians 3:13).
- Satan lost his authority to rule over you (Colossians 1:13).
- You have been given the authority to use the name of Jesus (Colossians 3:17).
- You have been given Christ's robe of righteousness (2 Corinthians 5:21).
- You are now a priest of God, set apart for his glory (1 Peter 2:5, 9).
- You were reborn into royalty, a child of God (John 1:12, Romans 8:16, and 1 John 3:2).
- You were chosen and adopted into royalty (Ephesians 1:5, Romans 8:15, and Galatians 4:7).
- You inherited royalty by conquest when Jesus triumphed over Satan (Colossians 2:15).

We must understand that God relates to us only through our sanctified spirit.

Our unsanctified soul once controlled us, but now our soul has to learn to take a back seat and let our born-again spirit rule. Our unsanctified memory in our soul might even question things, but it must be retrained by the Bible's message to us.

That's why we need to renew our mind by reading the Word of God and believing what it says about us. Jesus said in John 8:32, "And you shall know the truth, and the truth shall make you free." Therefore, biblical truth we know really brings freedom to us. Even in the Old Testament, we read in Proverbs 23:7, "As a man thinks in his heart, so is he."

If we place more importance on what others say instead of on what the Bible says or on our own understanding or feelings instead of what God says about us, we will never feel like winners.

We must change the way we think for our life to change. The Bible calls this process renewing the mind. (See Romans 12:1-2.)

Renewing our minds is a lifelong process. To do this, we must meditate or chew over the things we read in the Bible. We must claim for ourselves the promises that touch our spirits. When we worry about something, we repeatedly chew it over in our minds again and again. Adopt this same principle when it comes to God's Word, chewing it over again and again. This is called biblical meditation. Ask the Holy Spirit to give you his understanding as you read God's Word, and you will grow in faith. The New Age movement has adopted the word meditation, but Satan is behind New Age teachings. True biblical meditation will honor Almighty God.

We read in Romans 10:17 that "Faith comes by hearing, and hearing by the word of God." My Bible notes say, "Faith comes through hearing, and salvation comes through faith."[5]

God doesn't see your bodies as being either good or bad, for it just reacts to what is happening in the physical realm. Your earthly body is temporary, but your soul and spirit are eternal. They are the REAL you! Your soul also has a conscience, and when born-again believers listen to their conscience, God is very pleased.

We use our will in our soul to renew our thought life to line up with God's Word. The more we do this, the more Christ-like we become. We are constantly in touch with our soul, and we all express ourselves differently. Every born-again Christian has the resurrection life of God within their spirit. Yet at times, we can all feel depressed or angry in our soul. Even Jesus was sad and angry at times.

In Galatians 5:22, the apostle Paul has listed the wonderful fruit God has deposited into our born-again soul so that we can reflect his love to others. God wants us to release this fruit in our

---

[5] Hayford, *The New Spirit-Filled Life Bible*.

day-to-day lives. The nine fruit of the Spirit listed in these verses follow: "love, joy, peace, longsuffering, kindness, goodness, faithfulness, gentleness and self-control."

We must realize that we can't contact our spirit by our emotions or by our physical body as only the Word of God and the Spirit of God can touch our spirit.

We have already learned that everyone is born spiritually dead. But at salvation, our spirit was infused with God's Holy Spirit. At that instant, our human spirit in our inner soul was made absolutely perfect forever, but it takes a lifetime to transform our soul's way of thinking and behaving.

Ephesians 6:12-18 teaches that there is a constant spiritual war going on around us. Therefore, our spiritual growth depends on who is inwardly prompting us. These inner promptings come from either God's Kingdom or from Satan's kingdom. If you discern that they come from the devil, *then rebuke him out loud in the name of Jesus Christ* and tell him he is a liar and command him to depart from you. When you call on the name of Jesus Christ, he has to go!

**Matthew's Comments**
Many people, even those that are born again, don't know that they have three parts. Of course, if you mention a person's appetite and their desire for food and water as part of their bodily desires, they will understand what you mean. If you tell them that envy and jealousy are part of their soul and mind, they can grasp that also. But the fact remains that many people find it hard to feel their spirits. Your spirit is the part of you that desires more of God; your spirit desires the presence of God and his anointing.

Many people do not understand that their spirit has been perfected. Many of us struggle with sin, and if we are honest with ourselves, we consider ourselves sinners. But the Bible calls us righteous, complete, and whole. Our spirits are fully righteous and whole, and we just need to convert our souls—our mind, will and emotions—to the ways and means of God.

One major key to converting our minds and bodies and conforming them to God and his ways is for us to read and meditate on the Word of God. We should not be looking at others and comparing ourselves to them, but we should be looking to the Word of God and conforming ourselves to what it says. Reading the Word might not as be effective as pondering it for years. That is what my mother referred to as Christian meditation. In my own life, I have meditated on certain passages of scripture for twenty years and other scriptures, I have pondered for about six years. I have pondered different sections of the Bible for various amounts of time. I can see my life now conforming to those scriptures. Those passages are not just scripture anymore; they have become part of who I am.

Similarly, you should allow the Holy Spirit to highlight passages in the Bible to you, and you should ponder or meditate on those scriptures until they become living in you. That way, your soul will be conformed into the image of Christ.

# LESSON 5: JUSTICE, MERCY, TWO TYPES OF RIGHTEOUSNESS, AND THE ASSURANCE OF SALVATION

<u>JUSTICE AND MERCY</u>: No one can simultaneously act in both justice and mercy. To satisfy justice, sin must be punished, but when sin is forgiven, this demonstrates mercy. When Adam and Eve sinned, God exercised his justice. He had to because God is faithful to his word. Unlike us, God will not allow his emotions to deter him from doing what is right.

The only way that both justice and mercy can be fully satisfied is for an innocent third party to intervene. God knows the future, so when he created Adam and Eve, he already had plan B in mind, which was the heart-wrenching way of the cross.

The good news of the cross is that Christ Jesus took the collective sin of the whole world upon his own body and suffered the due penalty *on our behalf*! You and I didn't even exist back then, but the Father was exercising mercy to ALL mankind even though it broke his heart to see his own Son brutally suffer and die two thousand years later.

God couldn't ignore Adam's sin because God is holy. To ignore sin, he would not be acting justly, and worse still, he would have made himself a liar. God can't go back on his word. Years ago, I heard the following story that beautifully illustrates this predicament.

An army captain suspected that one of his men was a traitor because every day, the enemy seemed to know exactly what was ahead. The captain called a special parade. When his men were all assembled, the captain warned them that when the traitor was discovered, he would be tied to a post and flogged until he died.

A week passed. Then the captain was told that the traitor had been caught. To the captain's horror, it was his only son. What was he to do? He couldn't go back on his word. This loving father was absolutely devastated, but he eventually announced to his men, "The traitor has been discovered, and the flogging will take place at noon today."

His son was led to the flogging post, and his distraught father came and told the guards to release his son. He said, "I'm taking his place, and I order you to give my son the same privileges as all the other men." He then commanded his soldiers to begin the execution.

You see, the only way that both justice and mercy can be fully satisfied is for an innocent third party to lovingly step in and take the punishment for someone else's sin. That is exactly what God the Son did for us on the cross over two thousand years ago. Jesus, God the Son, took our sin upon himself so that we, the guilty ones, could go free. God not only made us, but he also died for us—so great is his love for all of us!

THE RIGHTEOUSNESS OF MAN: The Bible teaches that natural man has no self-righteousness, and we all need to have God's righteousness imputed to us before we die. This type of righteousness comes from God's grace alone, demonstrated on the cross of Jesus.

The Lord Jesus Christ on the cross has forever reconciled mankind to God. Together, he and his Son did everything possible to fix man's sin problem. Out of love for us, Jesus has already suffered the penalty for the whole world's collective sin. In response to his sacrifice, we all must personally acknowledge the Father's love gift. How? We are to prayerfully acknowledge our own sin to God and ask the Lord Jesus Christ to send the Holy Spirit into our life to be our new boss.

The problem man has is that we are used to fixing things ourselves. Our natural sin nature causes self-centeredness, which is inner pride. Pride then causes a person to feel or act self-righteously. "By pride comes nothing but strife, but with the well-advised is wisdom" (Proverbs 13:10). "Pride goes before destruction, and a haughty spirit before a fall" (Proverbs 16:18).

It's not so much what people do to us that causes anger to rise up within us. No, it's the self-centeredness and pride in our souls' emotions that manifest in anger. Self-pride is the cause of all contention. Jesus was never self-centered, but he did display righteous anger several times regarding his Father's house. Jesus made it very clear that what his Father honored was not to be abused.

Jesus was always more concerned about others than he was about himself. The reason why he could forgive and pray for others on the cross in the midst of intense agony proved beyond doubt that self-centeredness was not in his nature. True righteousness only comes from God.

We can never win God's acceptance by performing so-called good works because only God is good. Pride in our own self-achievement is arrogance. "A man's pride will bring him low, But the humble in spirit will retain honor" (Proverbs 29:23). A self-righteous person cannot be humble.

God hates religion in any form because religion is man's vain attempt to reach up to a holy God. Christianity alone recognizes that God in love reached down to sinful man. Father God fully approved of his Son's obedience by raising him from the dead. Over the centuries, skeptics have tried to disprove the bodily resurrection of Jesus only to come to the conclusion that they needed to surrender their life to the risen Lord Jesus Christ.

GOD'S GIFT OF RIGHTEOUSNESS: Every believer is freely given God's righteousness at the moment of salvation. They are accepted by the Father because of their faith in the death of Jesus for them. One dying thief confessed on the cross that he deserved to die, and Jesus immediately gave him the assurance of eternal life. Obviously, forgiveness was not based on works the man had done but on his humble attitude and his last-minute faith in the true identity of Jesus, who was dying right next to him. The other criminal had not repented of his sins and went to a lost eternity.

Having the gift of God's righteousness forever gives us right standing before the Father. "For He (the Father) made Him (Jesus) who knew no sin to be sin for us, that we might become the righteousness of God in Him" (2 Corinthians 5:21). Believers are to know with absolute confidence that Father God only sees them as totally acceptable because his blood has cleansed them from all sin—past, present, and future. It's a done deal—the last words of Jesus on the cross were "It is finished."

Although Jesus has forever conquered the sting of death, we each have to personally acknowledge his work. We are to:

1. Sincerely repent of all personal sin.
2. Ask for God's forgiveness.
3. Invite Jesus Christ into our life to be our Lord and Savior.

Jesus died for Adam's sin and the collective sin of mankind, but only those who personally place their faith in God's goodness as demonstrated on the cross of Jesus receive eternal forgiveness. Therefore, apathy, ignorance, or stubborn pride sends people to hell, not God.

Let's imagine that you were given a check to cash for a million dollars, but you just stored it as a keepsake in a drawer somewhere; the gift would be wasted. On the other hand, if you presented it to your bank, you would be a millionaire and the giver of the gift would be rewarded by witnessing your joy. In the same way, salvation is offered to the whole world, but we each need to respond to God's offer. Otherwise, we will miss out on all the benefits and eventually end up in a place we don't want to be.

The gift of righteousness can never be earned nor can this gift be accidentally lost. People might see themselves as Christians, but they have never repented nor been willing to make changes to their lifestyle. They just want the benefits of salvation. These people are deceived and need to be open to the full gospel message as God's Holy Spirit is not in them.

ASSURANCE OF SALVATION: God's Holy Spirit resides in every born-again person, and the righteousness of Christ covers them, so they automatically become a member of the royal household of God. These things happen silently and inwardly in the spiritual dimension, but mentally and emotionally, believers know that they have become new on the inside. They want to please God and are hungry to know more about him and the Bible. They also have the liberty to say, "The Lord is my helper; I will not fear. What can man do to me?" (Hebrews 13:5b-6).

On the night before the cross, Jesus prayed for his disciples and for all future believers. He then said to his Father, "I have glorified You on earth. I have finished the work which You have given Me to do. And now, O Father, glorify Me together with Yourself, with the glory which I had with You before the world was." (John 17:4-5).

Jesus wasn't on the cross at that point, so what was the finished work of Jesus on earth?

The verse above tells us that his mission on earth was to glorify his Father, which he had done. He continually demonstrated the true character of his Father to all those he met by word and action. Jesus was in constant communion with his Father, and he knew that he had finished his commission. He now only needed his Father's inner strength to surrender his life to the physical and spiritual torture of the cross for his time on earth was short.

Today, Father God wants everyone to come to him knowing that true love sacrificially gives out to others. As born-again Christians, we already have the fruit of the Spirit in us to enable us to love others, just like Jesus does. As I stated in Chapter 4, the fruit of the Spirit is "love, joy, peace, longsuffering, kindness, goodness, faithfulness, gentleness, and self-control" (Galatians 5:22-23).

Therefore, our mission on earth is to glorify God. We won't be crucified on a wooden cross as Jesus was, but we will be increasingly ridiculed by unbelievers for our Christian faith.

Morally, the world today is on a downward spiral and is rapidly becoming more anti-Christian. As the world flaunts their sinful ways, we are to be mindful that we are God's light to people everywhere. On earth, Jesus gained strength from his Father and the indwelling Holy Spirit to help him fulfill his mission. We need to be continually mindful that, as a child of God, we are to draw inner strength in the same way.

When a non-believer sees good fruit in our lives, they are more open to receive the Lord Jesus into their own life. Betty Jordon, my godly neighbor in Sydney, stirred up an inner jealousy in my heart. I wanted to be a good mother and train my child in the right way, but I didn't know the right way, and even if I did, I wouldn't be able to do it in my own strength.

Most issues in life are not eternally important, but we need to have absolute assurance about one vital issue. Ask yourself, "Am I a Christian? Do I know with an absolute certainty that I have eternal life? If I should die today, do I know without a doubt that I would go to heaven?"

God not only wants to save you, he wants us to know you are saved.

If you don't have the assurance of salvation, the devil will constantly bring condemnation to you. If you are a born-again Christian, then God the Holy Spirit now lives in your human spirit in your inner soul. Right now, one-third of you is absolutely perfect as God himself lives in you. Inwardly, you really do know that you are very different than you once were.

Don't let the devil tell you otherwise. Verbally rebuke his unspoken lies. "Be sober, be vigilant; because your adversary the devil walks about like a roaring lion, seeking whom he may devour" (1 Peter 5:8). Know that the devil has no authority in a believer's life except what we unknowingly give him.

An unbeliever might say, "I am a good person; I'll go to heaven." But God said, "We are all like an unclean thing and all our righteousnesses are like filthy rags" (Isaiah 64:6a). To God, human righteousness falls way short of God's righteousness. Salvation is a work of God. It is never a work of man. We read, "For by grace you have been saved through faith, and that not of yourselves; it is the gift of God, not of works, lest anyone should boast" (Ephesians 2:8-9).

Only our Lord Jesus Christ was born perfect and lived a perfect life. God's grace is often described as his unmerited favor toward a repentant sinner. God's grace actually empowers a Christian to live a God-pleasing life.

Some people might say, "No one can be sure about having eternal life." But Jesus said, "For God loved the world so much that He gave His only Son so that whoever believes in Him should not perish but have everlasting life" (John 3:16).

We can have eternal life in heaven, or we can refuse to believe God and have eternal life in hell. "He who has the Son has life; he who does not have the Son of God does not have life" (1 John 5:12).

The apostle Paul said in Romans 10:13, "For whoever calls on the name of the Lord shall be saved."

Jesus gave us an invitation in Revelation 3:20. "Behold I stand at the door and knock. If anyone hears My voice and opens the door, I will come in to him and dine with him, and he with Me."

In summary, please review the following points:

1. Everyone except our Lord Jesus has sinned. Even the Pope inherited a sin nature.
2. The penalty of sin is spiritual death; everyone needs salvation.
3. It is impossible to be saved by our good works.
4. God sent his Son, Jesus Christ, to die for our sins so that we can be forgiven and receive eternal life.
5. The only way to receive eternal life is to confess that we have sinned, to believe that Jesus died in our place, and to call upon him to save us.
6. God has revealed his way of salvation to us clearly in the Bible. Therefore, we can know with absolute certainty that we are saved and are part of the royal family of God.
7. When we humbly ask Jesus to save us, we receive three wonderful privileges:
   A. God's forgiveness of sin.
   B. The indwelling Holy Spirit.
   C. Eternal life.

**Matthew's Comments**

God did a wonderful thing through the death of Jesus to provide mercy for you and me. We must never forget that the death of Jesus and the shedding of his blood washed us clean and allowed us to become righteous before a holy God. We must not lose sight of the fact that Jesus did all the work and that his sacrifice alone saved us and not our own works.

I have to confess that it has been a constant struggle in my life to accept that I am saved through Jesus's death alone. I continue to live life by trying to impress God with what I do for him. I am constantly pushing myself to do good works. Of course, I do many of these works when the Holy Spirit has led and directed me, but I have to confess that some of the good things that I do have been done in my flesh. It's as though I don't feel worthy enough to go to heaven on the merits of Christ's death, and I seem to want to perform to ensure my salvation.

Is this also true of you in some way? Do you feel worthy of being saved, or do you think you have to do something to earn your salvation? Do you feel that you have to build up your works to ensure your salvation? This striving is no good. God does not like or approve of these works of self-righteousness. I only mention this in my life to help you identify this in your own life. The Bible calls this behavior of ours striving. We need to quit our striving and enter into the rest of the Lord. Read Hebrews 4 for more about entering the rest of the Lord.

# LESSON 6: WATER BAPTISM, INFANT DEDICATION, AND HOLY COMMUNION

At a wedding, a bride and groom publicly exchange wedding rings to symbolize their marriage. Likewise, water baptism is a symbol of salvation. Wearing a wedding ring doesn't make us married nor does water baptism save us. A wedding ring symbolizes a decision two people *have already made*, and water baptism symbolizes a decision a new believer *has already made*.

1. Water baptism is a public act that the Lord wants all believers to do as it expresses our faith in Jesus. Without that faith, the act means nothing. People who say no to water baptism are showing a dead faith to some extent. Faith is dead when people are unwilling to express it. James 2:26 says, "For as the body without the spirit is dead, so faith without works is dead also."

2. Water cannot wash away sin; only the blood of Jesus can do that. If you have repented of your sin and believe that Jesus died for you, then be baptized. This will demonstrate to God and to others the dramatic change that took place privately in your spirit when you invited Jesus Christ into your life as your personal Lord and Savior.

3. At water baptism, a believer is to be *fully submerged in water*. Going under the water signifies dying to Satan's kingdom, and coming up again signifies resurrection into God's kingdom. (See Matthew 3:16, Acts 8:36-39 and John 3:23.) The word baptize comes from the Greek *baptizo*, meaning to dip, dip under, dip in, sink, immerse, plunge, or cover wholly in liquid. The same word is used of dying garments.[6]

---

[6] "Baptizo," Bible Study Tools, Accessed February 5, 2018, https://www.biblestudytools.com/lexicons/greek/nas/baptizo.html.

4. Water baptism is the first public act of obedience that Jesus told believers to do. In a way, water baptism puts legs onto saving faith! Once, we were unknowing slaves of Satan, but at water baptism, we show God and other loved ones that we have come under a new and merciful Master.

5. Water baptism is evangelical, for we are encouraged to take the opportunity to briefly and publicly share with friends and family why we are being baptized. This outward physical evidence to others demonstrates that an inner change has already taken place in a person's life.

6. Water baptism should take place soon after salvation. (See Acts 2:38-41, Acts 16:14-15, and Acts 16:31-34.) By doing this, we are saying to the devil, "Satan, you and your demons are no longer my boss. I now belong to a wonderful new Master, the Lord Jesus Christ."

7. Every believer is to be baptized in the name of the Father, the Son, and the Holy Spirit, according to Matthew 28:19-20.

8. Water baptism is important because Jesus was baptized before he began his earthly ministry. If he submitted to water baptism, we should also.

Jesus said, "Go therefore and make disciples of all the nations, baptizing them in the name of the Father and of the Son and of the Holy Spirit, teaching them to observe all things that I have commanded you, and lo, I am with you always, even to the end of the age. Amen." (See Matthew 28:19-20 and Mark 16:16.)

When we asked Jesus into our life, our old sin nature died, and God's Holy Spirit entered our human spirit. Our human spirit, in our inner soul, was instantly perfected, and we received a brand-new identity. Rather than being separated from God, we became spiritually "in" Christ. The Holy Spirit in us is God's seal of ownership. "You were sealed with the Holy Spirit of promise, who is the guarantee of our inheritance, until the redemption of the purchased possession, to the praise of His glory" (Ephesians 1:13b-14).

The indwelling Holy Spirit is like God's deposit in us, signifying that he has already purchased us. His heavenly deposit in us could be compared to an earthly deposit we might make when we want to lay away goods at a store. These goods are deemed as ours even though they are still in the store. They become truly ours when we pay the balance owing.

In the same way, God has given us his Holy Spirit. One day in the future, he will come to take us home to live with him in heaven. This holy transaction happened spiritually between you and God when you inwardly accepted Jesus as your personal Lord and Savior.

If you are a believer but haven't been water-baptized, God wants you to make a decision to do so. Faith saves, but saving faith is never alone, for faith and action go together. The apostle Paul taught, "If you confess with your mouth the Lord Jesus and believe in your heart that God has raised Him (Jesus) from the dead, you will be saved" (Romans 10:9). Believing takes faith, but our confession of faith requires action.

As a believer, we have God's Holy Spirit in our human spirit. Therefore, our spirit can live outside time and space. The Bible tells us that our spirit is joined with Christ in heaven, and at the same time, it is in us on earth because God can be everywhere at the same time! Ephesians 2:5b-6 says that God "made us alive together with Christ (by grace you have been saved), and raised us up together, and made us sit together, in the heavenly places in Christ Jesus."

This is our *spiritual* position even though our body and soul are confined to earth until Jesus comes and takes us to himself. At salvation, we were also spiritually baptized into the "universal body of believers in Christ." All Christians belong to the huge family of God.

Regardless of what denomination we are, we are to model Jesus who humbled himself and washed his disciple's feet. He was Almighty God, and yet he had a servant's heart. Therefore, we are to see ourselves as humble servants of Christ. Though we live on earth, God now sees us as heavenly beings, and our character should align with his servant-like character.

INFANT DEDICATION: The baptism of a very young child who has no knowledge of God or sin is not biblical. Rather this type of service is really a dedication service *for the parents to promise to raise their child in a godly manner*. Be assured that every young child goes to heaven if they die because in God's sight, they are totally innocent of personal sin.

Believers are encouraged to bring their young children to their local church and dedicate themselves to their role as godly parents. Every parent really needs divine help to raise their children in a God-fearing manner, a reverent respect for God's holiness and goodness.

HOLY COMMUNION: This was set up by God for born-again believers. Therefore, it is not to be taken lightly or out of ignorance. Holy communion is an ongoing remembrance celebration for the work of the cross. We need to be continually reminded and eternally thankful for God's extravagant grace and love for us, demonstrated by our Lord Jesus Christ.

The Lord Jesus himself is the one mediator between us and Father God (1Timothy 2:5). Christ's work as high priest has forever replaced the Old Testament priesthood who made regular sacrifices year after year. As believers, "we are the royal priesthood of God." (See 1 Peter 2:9.) In Hebrews 4:16, we are told to come boldly into God's throne room as we pray to him, for his door is always open.

Communion is a time of personal reflection. It's the perfect time to confess sin to God and to receive healing from him. In Luke 22:15-20, Jesus said to his twelve apostles, "'With fervent desire I have desired to eat this Passover with you before I suffer; for I say to you, I will no longer eat of it until it is fulfilled in the kingdom of God.'

"Then He took the cup, and gave thanks, and said, 'Take this and divide among yourselves; for I say to you, I will not drink of the fruit of the vine until the kingdom of God comes.'

"And then He took the bread and gave thanks and broke it, and gave it to them saying, 'This is My body which is given for you; do this in remembrance of Me.' Likewise He also took the cup after supper saying, 'This cup is the new covenant in My blood, which is shed for you.'"

There has been some confusion here about the meaning of this passage. Bread and wine do not become the literal body and blood of Jesus as some leaders teach. The words, "this is my blood," don't mean exactly the same. I can show you a picture of my mother and say, "That's my Mom!" But it's only an image of her, a metaphor. When Jesus said, "I am the vine," he didn't mean that he was a literal vine!

But he is the door to God that we must go through, for he said, "I am the door. If anyone enters by Me, he will be saved, and will go in and out and find pasture. The thief does not come except to steal, and to kill, and to destroy. I have come that they may have life, and that they may have it more abundantly (John 10:9-10).

Our Lord has instructed us to regularly participate in the communion service because we need to be continually reminded of the love of God and the extravagant cost of our salvation. We are not to take these things lightly. Communion is a precious time for Christ's church to reflect on God's incredible grace. It is a time to openly thank him as a body of believers for his great sacrifice.

Jesus knew that his time on earth was almost over, and he was anticipating on-going spiritual communion with his saints. After the resurrection, the early church celebrated communion in their homes whenever they met together. (See Acts 2:42.)

Today at church, intimacy is still being built up between us as the Bride of Christ and our divine lover. Therefore, regular partaking of communion is particularly special to God and should be for us also. The term Bride of Christ refers to every born-again believer: men and women and boys and girls from all nations in the world. (See Ephesians 5:22-33.)

Communion requires spiritual intimacy between us and God.

1 Corinthians 11:27-29 says, "Therefore whoever eats this bread or drinks this cup of the Lord in an unworthy manner, will be guilty of the body and blood of the Lord. But let a man examine himself, and so let him eat of the bread and drink of the cup. For he who eats and drinks in an unworthy manner eats and drinks judgment to himself, not discerning the Lord's body."

Satan might put into your mind that you are not worthy to take communion. But if you are a born-again believer, then verbally rebuke Satan! Take communion with an open heart of thanksgiving and worship. You will be cleansed from the guilt that Satan wanted to burden you with. The devil always wants to keep us in bondage and fear so as to rob us of God's peace. If, however, the Holy Spirit nudges you with guilt, then confess it to God and receive his forgiveness. Then partake of communion.

Some versions of the New Testament translate the word unworthy as irreverently. The apostle Paul knew this for in 1 Corinthians 11:21-22, he condemned the early church for taking the communion wine and getting drunk on it and taking the communion bread and greedily making a meal out of it.

Communion is a time to intimately meet with Jesus and be cleansed. Jesus said, "I am the living bread which came down from heaven. If anyone eats of this bread, he will live forever; and the bread that I shall give is My flesh, which I shall give for the life of the world" (John 6:51). Jesus went into more detail about this in John 6:53-57.

Later in John 6:66, we are told that many people no longer followed Jesus. We must realize that Jesus was not telling his followers to act like cannibals and literally eat his flesh and drink his blood. No! Jesus was using the terms symbolically. He simply wants us to believe in him and to eat and drink reverently at the Communion table. Just like the manna from heaven, Jesus is our provider; abide in him. Communion is a believer's soul food.

At the last Passover, Jesus said that he would not partake of Communion again until he does so in heaven, celebrating with us at the Marriage Supper of the Lamb. In the meantime, he has commanded us to eat and to drink reverently, as part of his body of believers.

God sees our celebration of the work of the cross at communion as being as precious to him as a man and a woman committing their lives to each other in marriage. God wanted a huge family to pour his love onto. The idea of marriage is between a man and a woman who would joyfully share ongoing physical, emotional, and spiritual intimacy so that multiplication would result.

In God's sight, if there is no consummation of a marriage, there is no marriage, for that is where intimacy is built. Even our legal system will dissolve a marriage if it has not been consummated. In God's eyes, the begetting of children is important.

In violation of God's holy law, Australia's new law on marriage has been passed by the will of man as it is totally opposed to the will of God. The United States passed a similar law some years ago.

Just as we are not to enter marriage lightly nor are we to take part in the communion service in a flippant manner. Both marriage and communion calls for serious personal reflection on our part as these celebration services are holy in God's sight. Communion is a time of personal intimacy with God, for in his eyes, the universal Church is the Bride of Christ, whether we are single or married, male or female.

NOTE: Contrary to Australia's new law on marriage, God will always see marriage as a sacred union between one man and one woman who wish to share ongoing physical and emotional intimacy together.

God told his people in Leviticus 18:22, "You shall not lie with a male as with a woman. It is an abomination." Again in Leviticus 20:13, God said, "If a man lies with a male as he lies with a woman, both of them have committed an abomination. They shall surely be put to death. Their blood shall be upon them." Read Romans 1:22-27 about this subject. My Bible notes say, "From a biblical standpoint, the rise of homosexuality is a sign that a society is in the last stages of decay."[7]

**Matthew's Comments**
I was twenty-seven years of age and at a church with a baptism service where about eight people were being baptized. As they were being baptized, I felt this tremendous peace of God. I looked up toward heaven where the joy and peace were coming from, and I saw the roof of the church open. I had a vision of Jesus in heaven, standing up in front of his throne, and he said, "Matthew, can you feel the joy here in heaven at this baptism service?"

I replied, "Yes, I feel that."

He said, "We are having a party up here. Matthew, I want you to get baptized, and I want you to win people to me and baptize them in my name."

---

[7] Hayford, *The New Spirit-Filled Life Bible*.

I had grown up in a Baptist church, and before you were baptized, you had to share a little of your testimony. I had such a fear of public speaking that this had prevented me from being baptized until that point. When Jesus told me in that vision to be baptized, I made it a priority and was baptized six weeks later.

I want to share a little on communion. You might have had communion so many times that the practice might have become mundane to you. You should take this to prayer so that you receive a fresh view of communion. Taking communion without thankfulness for the death of Jesus for your sake will not benefit you. This has happened to me before.

One time, I had dinner with a homeless man, and he removed some wine and bread. We had a very deep and personal communion. That was the sweetest time that I ever had during communion. The memory is so precious to me. It is okay for you to admit that communion has lost its appeal to you. If this is the case, God can change your heart and restore your love for communion and your intimacy with him.

# LESSON 7: THE BIBLE AND FULFILLED OLD TESTAMENT PROPHECIES

At salvation, God gave us an inbuilt desire to know more about him and the Christian life. He wants us to continually hunger for his written Word so that we can witness his love to others. Each week at church, we receive teaching on the Bible, but we are not meant to live on one spiritual meal a week. Our born-again spirit in our soul hungers for *daily spiritual food* so that our will, our emotions, and our thoughts can be transformed to the perfect will of God.

About four thousand years ago, God called Moses to bring his people out of slavery to the cruel Egyptians. The Israelites walked through the wilderness for forty years, and God continually sustained their bodies, their clothes, and footwear. He must have caused their clothing and footwear to increase in size, for they didn't wear out. (This was an ongoing miracle in itself.)

God fed them food from heaven called manna. This fresh food lay on the ground each morning, and his people collected enough for that day's need. If they collected more than they needed, the excess turned rotten. Every day, God's food totally sustained them, but their fallen human nature caused them to constantly complain to Moses.

Today, we have God's Word to spiritually sustain our human soul. Like the fresh manna given to the Israelites each day, we need to feed our soul on God's word every day. Let's do a Bible study together on 2 Timothy 3:15-17.

"And that from childhood you have known the Holy Scriptures, which are able to make you wise for salvation through faith which is in Christ Jesus. All Scripture is given by inspiration of God, and is profitable for doctrine, for reproof, for correction, for instruction in righteousness, that the man of God may be complete, thoroughly equipped for every good work."

1) What is the purpose of the Bible? See verse 15.

_____
_____
_____
_____

2) Who is the author of the Bible? See verse 16.

_____
_____

3) How much of the Bible is inspired?

_____
_____

4) What four things is the Bible profitable for? See question 6 below for the answers.

_____
_____
_____
_____
_____

5) How well prepared for life will the Bible make a person? See verse 17.

_____
_____

6) In verse 16, we learn that the Bible is profitable for four things. The meaning of each of these follows:
    A. Doctrine means teaching on how we should live.
    B. Reproof means rebuke. If we get off track, the Bible convicts us of this.
    C. Correction means that the Bible shows us how to get back on the right path once again.

D. Instruction in righteousness is the constant application of God's Word that will eventually train us in such a way that our lives become structured in righteous living.

7) What can the Bible do for us according to Psalm 119:9, 11, 105, 130, and 133?

v. 9

_____
_____

v. 11

_____
_____

v. 105

_____
_____

v. 130

_____
_____

v. 133

_____
_____

God wants us to get as much as possible out of a passage of Scripture, so try to establish a set time each day to read the Bible. Jesus taught us to pray, "Give us this day our daily bread." (See Matthew 6:11.) Choose a time and place where you are least likely to be interrupted and be assured that God wants to speak to you as you study his Word.

If you can, start the day by reading his Word, for it will better equip you to cope if problems occur. Or try to read before you are too tired to concentrate in the evening. If you miss a day, don't allow the devil to rob you of God's peace, for he knew your busy schedule in advance.

Ask God to give you understanding, for the Bible is not like other books. It was inspired by God the Holy Spirit although it was penned by holy men of God. (See 2 Peter 1:20 and 2 Timothy 3:16.)

Come to the Bible with a positive attitude, come in humility, and come to be changed by his Word. Most importantly, come to the Word in faith, believe it, and obey what God is convicting you of. Human wisdom falls way short of God's wisdom, so before you begin to read your Bible, take time to ask God to speak to your soul by giving you personal revelation about his written Word.

Learn to meditate or think about the passage and challenge yourself by going over and over something that seems difficult. It's better to read a little and have God speak to you than to read more without any real blessing from God. Ask these questions when you read:

- Is there a *command* I need to obey?
- Is there a *promise* I can trust in?
- Is there an *example* I can follow?
- Is there a *warning* I should heed?

Keep an exercise book or journal to jot down the date of your reading and anything you have learned that you could apply in your life, including any verses you found helpful. After a time when you look back on your notes, you will be surprised at how much you have grown.

Read James 1:22-25. "But be doers of the word, and not hearers only, deceiving yourselves. For if anyone is a hearer of the word and not a doer, he is like a man observing his natural face in a mirror; for he observes himself, goes away, and immediately forgets what kind of man he was. But he who looks into the perfect law of liberty and continues in it, and is not a forgetful hearer but a doer of the work, this one will be blessed in what he does."

Answer the following questions.

*What should we do* when we read truth? (v. 22)

_____

_____

If we read or hear truth, *but don't apply it*, what happens?

_____

_____

What danger does verses 23-24 speak of?

_____

_____

If we read and obey God's Word, what promise is given in verse 25?

_____

_____

The Bible is made up of sixty-six books written over fifteen hundred years by forty authors from three continents: Asia, Africa and Europe. The Old Testament was written in the Hebrew and Aramaic languages while the New Testament was written in Greek. Today, the Bible has been translated into every major world language. The Bible also is a "living" book as it constantly changes lives. More copies of the Bible have been sold than any other printed book!

No other book stirs up unbelievers like the Bible, for it opens with, "In the beginning God created the heavens and the earth" (Genesis 1:1). This brings heated debate, for it claims that all creation, visible and invisible, is the result of the Creator's handiwork, and the earth didn't just evolve from nothing!

Most importantly, the Bible reveals that God yearns for us to have a personal relationship with him. He has done all he can to bring this about, but we must personally respond to his love.

At birth, we had everything we needed for adulthood; we just needed time to grow into it. In the physical world, it's a tragedy if a baby doesn't grow to maturity. This is also true of "baby" Christians. They might have known the Lord for years but have become lazy in maintaining their walk with God. Just like our body, we need to keep our soul clean for God.

At our spiritual rebirth, we received the Holy Spirit into our life, and over time, we will learn to grow into the person God has designed us to be. Gradually, we will grow in the knowledge of God and will learn and experience even more of his goodness to us. God *loves* to listen as we talk to him, and he wants us to take the time to *listen to him* when he speaks to us!

The Bible contains history, prophecy, poetry, and instructions for living. One compelling story and one solution is woven throughout the entire book. The main theme of the entire Bible is the cross of Jesus and what that means for both believers and unbelievers today.

The Bible alone creates faith in God! "Faith comes by hearing, and hearing by the word of God" (Romans 10:17). Without the help of the Holy Spirit, the Bible seems boring and irrelevant. That's why unbelievers think that it's rubbish just as I once did, but now I realize that there are five compelling reasons why we can believe that the Bible is, in fact, God's Word to mankind.

1. REASON DEMANDS IT. We are the treasured creation of God. Therefore, it stands to reason that our Creator would give us his instruction manual for successful living. Even a human manufacturer wants his products cared for, so he

places a manual with the product. How much more does our loving Father want us to have a complete guide for living and directions on how to have a meaningful relationship with him?

2. HISTORY CONFIRMS IT. The wonder of the Bible doesn't simply stand on its moral teachings, but the Bible provides facts for our faith. No other history book has been tested as much as the Bible. This book alone claims to be the Word of God. Jesus Christ is the only religious leader in the whole world who actually claimed to BE God and could support his claim by performing miracles, even raising three people from the dead. Later, he rose from the dead and was physically seen by reliable witnesses.

3. ARCHAEOLOGY SUPPORTS IT. No discovery has ever disproved statements in Scripture. Every Christian can take the whole Bible in their hand and say without fear or hesitation that he holds the true Word of God, handed down without essential loss from generation to generation throughout many centuries.

4. CHRIST CONFIRMED IT. Even though Jesus only had the Old Testament at the time, Jesus quoted it and taught it as truth to his disciples. Jesus didn't even argue with Satan when the devil tried to test him. He simply quoted scriptures from Deuteronomy and Psalms. God's Word silenced Satan back then, and it does the same today! The Old Testament points to the New Testament while the New Testament is better understood because of some of the challenging teachings in the Old Testament.

5. PROPHECY PROVES IT. The greatest proof that the Bible was inspired by God's Spirit is the number of prophecies in it that have been fulfilled. God alone knows the future. Therefore, he can, without fail, predict future events. Almost one third of all Bible content is prophecy. With this lesson, I have enclosed a separate sheet which lists thirty of

the three hundred fulfilled prophecies, taken from Isaiah and Psalms.

God wants us to truly meditate on the Bible. For example, when you mull over a problem in your mind, it's called worry. When you think about a Bible verse over and over in your mind, it's called meditation. The more you meditate on Scripture, the less you have to worry about! In other words, prayer is speaking to God; meditation allows God to speak to you. That's why *slowly reading the Bible* is far more productive than reading it like a novel.

Learn to love what God loves and to hate what God hates, for this is the "fear of the Lord," and it's the beginning of wisdom. (See Proverbs 9:10.) Those who fear the Lord are truly God's intimate friends. This type of fear is not a scary sort of fear but a deep love and reverence for God. Part of this process is to ask God to help you to "turn away your eyes from looking at worthless things" (Psalm 119:37a). Therefore, we are to be aware of what we allow our eyes to see, our ears to listen to, and what words we use.

**Prophecies of Isaiah 700 years before Christ N.T. Fulfillment**

He (Immanuel) will be born of a virgin

(Isaiah 7:14) Matthew 1:23

He will be the Prince of Peace

(Isaiah 9:6-7) John 14:27

He will be exalted

(Isaiah 52:13) Philippians 2:9

He will be widely rejected

(Isaiah 53:3) John 12:37-38

He will bear our sins and sorrows

(Isaiah 53:4) Rom. 4:25, 1 Peter 2:24-25

He will make a blood atonement

(Isaiah 53:5) Romans 3:25

He will be our substitute

(Isaiah 53:6, 8) 2 Corinthians 5:21

He will not defend himself

(Isaiah 53:7) Matthew 27:12-14

He will voluntary accept our guilt and punishment

(Isaiah 53:7) John 10:11

He will be buried in a rich man's tomb

(Isaiah 53:9) Matthew 27:57-60

He will justify many from their sin

(Isaiah 53:10-11) Romans 5:15-19

He will die with transgressors

(Isaiah 53:12) Mark 15:27-28, Luke 22:37

**Prophecies in Psalms 1,000 years before Christ N. T. Fulfillment**

The Son of God

(Psalms 2:6-7) Matthew 3:17

Ruler of all

(Psalms 8:6) Hebrews 2:8; 1 Cor.15:25; Matthew 28:18

Rises from death

(Psalms 16:10) Matthew 28:7

Ridiculed by his enemies

(Psalms 22:7-8) Luke 23:35

Hands and feet pierced
(Psalms 22:16) John 20:27
Lots cast for clothes
(Psalms 22:18) Matthew 27:35
Bones unbroken
(Psalms 34:20) John 19:32-33, 36
Hated without cause
(Psalms 35:19) John 15:24-25
Delights in God's will
(Psalms 40:7-8) Hebrews 10:7
Betrayed by a friend
(Psalms 41:9) Luke 22:47-48
The eternal King
(Psalms 45:6) Hebrews 1:8
Ascends to heaven and frees captives
(Psalms 68:18) Acts 1:9-11; Eph. 4:8
Zealous for God's house
(Psalms 69:9) John 2:16-17
Given vinegar and gall
(Psalms 69:21) Matthew 27:34
Rules over his enemies
(Psalms 110:1) Matt. 22:44; Hebrews 1:13
A priest forever
(Psalms 110:4) Hebrews 5:6

The chief cornerstone of God's building
(Psalms 118:22) Matthew 21:42
Comes in the name of the Lord
(Psalms 118:26) Matthew 21:9

# LESSON 8: FELLOWSHIP WITH GOD AND WITH OTHER BELIEVERS

We know from reading John 4:23-24 that Jesus wants us to worship him in spirit and in truth. Insincere praise is an insult to God! "Man looks on the outward appearance but the Lord looks at the heart" (1 Samuel 16:7).

FELLOWSHIP WITH GOD: To fully identify with us, Jesus lived on earth as a Spirit-filled human being. He therefore had to constantly communicate with his Father, for as a human, he needed his Father's directions and strength as he preached and performed mighty miracles.

In Mark 2, we see that in just one day, Jesus chose his first four disciples, taught in the synagogue, cast out a demon, and healed Peter's mother-in-law. Later after supper, the whole city gathered at his door, so he went out and ministered to all their needs. Finally, he collapsed into bed, but he arose before sunrise in order to spend time in prayer in a solitary place (Mark 1:35). Later in Luke 11:1-4, the disciples asked him *to teach them how to pray*, for they had obviously linked his commitment to his prayer life to his extraordinary ministry power.

God's wants to mold every believer into the image of Jesus. Often we ask God to change negative situations or to change other people when actually these very things are often used by God to change us. Over time and with God's help, we will change our thoughts and actions, depending on how close our relationship is with Jesus.

In prayer, continually praise God for his intervention in your life and constantly thank him for listening to your prayers. When you realize how much he has changed you, your confidence for answered prayers will increase. Bear in mind always that prayer and praise are extremely powerful tools to use against the kingdom of darkness as many of Satan's captives can be set free by genuine prayers that God will intervene in their lives.

Draw close to God and claim his protection over loved ones, confidently knowing that "He is near to all who call upon Him . . . . He will hear their cry and save them" (Psalm 145:18a, 19b). Our prayers are so very precious to God. Even if we don't FEEL like praying, confess this to him and start praying anyway, for soon the emotion will follow. Satan is not the only one who stops us from praying as often the old patterns in our minds will battle our born-again spirit. Therefore by faith, earnestly ask the Holy Spirit to help you pray.

Ephesians 6:12 teaches us that we are in spiritual warfare with demons. Praise to our Heavenly Father is our best weapon against demons, for they hate to hear us praising God. When the Israelites went into battle, the priests and worshippers led their army by joyfully singing praises to Jehovah. They knew from experience that this would ensure victory in battle (2 Chronicles 20:22).

Today, nothing has changed; God loves to dwells in our praise, according to Psalm 22:3. To him, praise is worship because it causes our thoughts and emotions to come into line with our born-again spirit. Paul said, "I urge you, brothers and sisters, in view of God's mercy, to offer your bodies as a living sacrifice, holy and pleasing to God – this is your true and proper worship" (Romans 12:1, NIV). This type of praying is also warfare against self-centeredness, for it frees God to act in the situation on our behalf.

Although the Holy Spirit helps us to pray, we are to always pray to Father God through the mighty name of Jesus. The whole Trinity should be involved. Try to establish a daily prayer time that you and God can look forward to. But don't become legalistic. Otherwise, the devil will put guilt onto you if something prevents you from praying.

Be mindful that you will be meeting with the Lord God in heaven, so take time to sense his holy presence. For the first few minutes, don't ask for anything, just praise him for who he is by worshipping him and thanking him for all the wonderful blessings he has already given to you. Tell him how much you love and appreciate him. Be real with him; share your concerns and thank him in advance for answered prayer.

God doesn't need long or fancy prayers because he is your heavenly Dad! Besides, he already knows your needs, but he rejoices in your faith in him to supply them. He values your affection and heart attitude more than anything else. Although we know that God *can* answer our prayer, we often doubt whether he *will*. God answers prayers of faith, for Jesus said, "According to your faith let it be to you." (See Matthew 8:13 and 9:29, NIV).

Know that when we doubt God's goodness, we may negate our prayer. "He who doubts is like a wave of the sea driven and tossed by the wind. For let not that man suppose that he will receive anything from the Lord; he is a double-minded man, unstable in all his ways" (James 1:6b-8).

Satan hates prayer and does everything he can to stop us from praying. He wants to destroy our faith in God's goodness to us, just like he did with Eve in the garden. Stand firm in Jesus's name and actively resist the lies that the devil plants in your mind. Stay grounded in God's Word. "God is not a man that He should lie, nor a son of man, that He should repent. Has He said, and will He not do? Or has He spoken, and will He not make it good?" (Numbers 23:19).

Powerful believers never doubt God's goodness. Therefore, God can do mighty miracles through them. Jesus said, "Whatever things you ask when you pray, believe that you receive them, and you will have them" (Mark 11:24b). Know that time often lags between God's answer and the manifestation of his answer! In the case of the fig tree, the roots began to die when Jesus cursed the tree, but it took time for the death process to manifest above the ground. This story assures us that the believing prayer of faith is settled in heaven when we pray, but the physical evidence seen by us can often be a process.

We are to never forget that believers have open access to God's throne room. The following verses that have helped me in my prayer life are all about knowing Jesus.

- "He who calls you is faithful, who also will do it" (1 Thessalonians 5:24).
- "For I know whom I have believed and am persuaded that He is able to keep what I have committed to Him until that Day" (2 Timothy 1:12b).
- "Looking unto Jesus, the author and finisher of our faith" (Hebrews 12:2a).

When Jesus was on earth, he continually prayed for strength from his Father, and he was not disappointed. Today as followers of Christ, we can be confident that God wants to strengthen us in our prayer life as well. More than anyone, Jesus understands human weakness, but he wants us to "come boldly to the throne of grace, that we may obtain mercy and find grace to help in our time of need" (Hebrews 4:16).

God encourages us to be frank and honest with him when we pray. Confess to him if you hold resentments or disappointments and let him lift your burden. Jesus said, "Come to Me, all you who labor and are heavy laden, and I will give you rest. Take My yoke upon you and learn from Me, for I am gentle and lowly in heart, and you will find rest for you souls. For My yoke is easy and My burden is light" (Matthew 11:28-30).

God's chief aim is to mold us into the image of his Son. We often ask God to resolve negative situations or to change other people when actually those very situations are often used by him to change us. Over time with God's help, we can change our own mindsets but not the mindsets of others. But in prayer, God might change others. He changed my faithless heart, so I know that if someone is regularly prayed for, God can change them!

Prayer and praise are powerful spiritual weapons to use against the kingdom of darkness. Believers can set Satan's captives free just by praying that God will intervene in their lives. In the meantime, draw close to God and claim his protection over loved ones.

We might genuinely want to draw close to God, but from his viewpoint, he is never far away from any of us. "The Lord is near to all who call upon Him . . . . He also will hear their cry and save them" (Psalm 145:18a, 19b).

"Call to Me, and I will answer you, and show you great and mighty things, which you do not know" (Jeremiah 33:3). This verse is divine revelation and spiritual faith warfare. In fact, I have a note next to this verse in my Bible, saying that on September 7, 2007, I stood up in church and claimed it for my mother's salvation. A year later, God confirmed to me that he would save her.

If you don't feel like praying, confess this to God and start praying anyway. Soon the emotion will follow. The old patterns in your mind try to fight your born-again spirit, but don't give in. Begin to pray about the situation and ask God to help you.

- Ephesians 6:12 tells us that we are in spiritual warfare.
- Praise is our weapon against the devil. It's the believer's battle banner of victory, according to 2 Chronicles 20:22.
- Know that God dwells in our praise. See Psalm 22:3.
- Praise is worship to God.

Praise will bring our emotions and our will into line with our born-again spirit. Paul said, "I urge you, brothers and sisters, in view of God's mercy, to offer your bodies as a living sacrifice, holy and pleasing to God – this is your true and proper worship" (Romans 12:1, NIV).

Insisting on our own way often blocks God's perfect will from happening. Know too, that offering ourselves to God in prayer is actually warfare against self-centeredness. The Holy Spirit in us wants us to be a "living sacrifice, holy and pleasing to God." We must be consciously aware of God's presence by faith even when we cannot feel his presence.

Although God is invisible, he has promised, "'I will never leave you nor forsake you.' So we may boldly say 'The Lord is my helper; I will not fear. What can man do to me?'" (Hebrews 13:5b-6). Thank him for all his promises to you.

FELLOWSHIP WITH OTHER BELIEVERS: Christ's church is a gathering of believers who meet in a church, a home, or anywhere else. In fact, *wherever* two or more believers meet, even on the street for a quick chat, the church of Christ enjoys fellowship.

Collectively, Christians worldwide are known as the universal church of God. We are also called the Bride of Christ in Revelation 21:2 and the Body of Christ, of which Jesus is the head. See Ephesians 1:22-23 and 1 Corinthians 12:27.

The apostle Paul said in 1 Corinthians 12:12-26 that Christ's church is meant to function like the human body. Just as our organs need each other, so too, do individual believers need each other. If we are careless about church fellowship, the whole body suffers. Our combined gifting and backgrounds make the church strong and healthy.

- The church is to pull together by sharing fellowship, worship, and praise.
- As a body of believers, we must work together and share the workload when possible.
- We are to joyfully contribute to the running costs just like any healthy grown-up family.
- We are to be God's light shining in a dark world (Philippians 2:14-16).
- Most importantly, the worldwide church is to be centered on the lordship of Jesus Christ.

Our relationships toward others have always been God's top concern. Our brothers and sisters in Christ are our spiritual family, so we must pull together and show love to one another. Love needs to be tested in order to mature! Therefore, the church is God's training ground to teach us how to love the way Jesus has commanded us in John 13:34. If we can't wholeheartedly love our own brothers and sisters in the Lord, how can we possibly love the people in the world like Jesus loves them?

God is more concerned about our character than our personal comfort. In fact, he often uses the personality of others to fine-tune our character. Every healthy church is made up of all the different character traits. We easily warm up to most people, but some might be a little prickly or irritating. Just use more of God's grace, and in time, you will come to enjoy their company.

God doesn't want us to be a bunny believer who hops around from church to church without serious commitment. Otherwise, God will only have to repeat the lesson you might be resisting. There is no such thing as a perfect church because we are all called to love imperfect people just like God does.

Mark 8:29 records a time when Jesus asked his disciples, "Who do you say I am?" and Peter responded, "You are the Christ, the Son of the living God." Jesus knew that Peter had received revelation from Father God in heaven, and he promised to build his church, and the gates of hell would not prevail against it. (My Bible notes say, "This incident took place six months before the crucifixion. It was pivotal in Jesus's ministry, marking the climax of his teaching concerning his own Person. Jesus then began preparing his disciples for his approaching death.)[8]

Just like the home, the government, or the workplace, a line of authority exists in the local church, and if we resist it, we are resisting God himself (Romans 13:1-2). Our spiritual growth slows down if we start finding fault with others. Both Colossians 3:12-13

---

[8] Hayford, *The New Spirit-Filled Life Bible*.

and Philippians 2:3-4 instruct us to exercise forgiveness and humility, knowing that reconciliation is made possible through Christ who forgave us. We forgive others as a conscious choice so that we will not hold an offense organized by Satan against others.

Pastors have the awesome responsibility of protecting and feeding God's children. Therefore, we are to know that they are not answerable to us but to God alone. We are told to "obey those who rule over you, and be submissive, for they watch out for your souls, as those who must give account. Let them do so with joy and not with grief, for that would be unprofitable for you" (Hebrews 13:17).

Our enemy is Satan, not people! (Ephesians 6:12). Satan throws us rotten bait called offenses. If someone picks them up, things like gossip, division, and pride will begin to destroy relationships, causing people to backslide or to leave the church very disgruntled.

Instead, we must constantly focus on the love of God and pray for the whole fellowship, especially the leaders. Holding onto offense prevents unbelievers from being saved and believers from growing. When others say or do hurtful things, we MUST forgive them and move on. Also, if we take on someone else's offense, we become the devil's next victim.

It's amazing, but when you start to regularly pray for someone, you see things in their life that are positive, and you wonder why you ever had a problem with them. Instead of gossiping to others, tell God about personality issues. Then he is free to work on your behalf. If we insist on reacting in our flesh, God's hands are tied, and the whole church suffers.

We are to realize that we are a mixed bunch of people all trying to retrain fleshly minds. Many people stumble and need help. Some are babies, needing extra attention and patience. Others might carry very heavy baggage. 1 Peter 4:8 says, "Have fervent love for one another, for love will cover a multitude of sins."

Christ's church is to be committed to pull together in all the ups and downs of growing, for it is God the Holy Spirit—not us—who does the mighty work of transforming sinners into saints.

A common story in Christian circles follows.

A pastor went to visit a man who had been absent from church for some time. It was bitterly cold, and when he arrived, he found the man huddled near the fireplace. The pastor silently sat on a chair opposite him. No one spoke although the man guessed the purpose of the visit.

A short time passed, and the pastor leaned forward and removed a burning ember with the fire tongs and placed it on the hearth, then silently sat back again. After a few minutes, the ember had stopped glowing. It lay cold and dead on the hearth. The pastor looked at the ember, then looked at the man, rose to his feet, and said. 'Thank you for your time. Goodbye.'

The man replied, 'Thank you for your visit, Pastor, particularly for your fiery sermon. I will be back at church on Sunday.'

Without even speaking a word, the pastor had preached his best message on the importance of regular church attendance. As long as the log was in the fire with the other logs, it burned brightly. Each burning log helped the others to burn bright. Once the log was taken out of the fire and was alone, it quickly went out. Christianity is exactly like that."

The moral of the story is that Christians are not meant to live in isolation from other believers. We need to participate in regular church fellowship. Some believers think that they can remain strong without leaving their home, but God knows we need each other because we have a common enemy who wants to devour us. "Be careful—watch out for attacks from Satan, your great enemy. He prowls around like a hungry, roaring lion, looking for some victim to tear apart" (1 Peter 5:8, TLB).

God wants to enlarge his Kingdom, and every believer has their role to play. The church is our training ground to reach out in love to others. People are surprised if you ask them home for lunch. If they can't come for some reason, ask them if they can come the following week. *But don't make a big deal of what to feed them. Just prepare something easy*, like a bowl of soup or sandwiches. By keeping it simple, they will realize that they too can reach out to people in this way. *God wants us to demonstrate friendliness.*

**Matthew's Comments**
Reading the Word of God is vital. Most of the time, you will need more scripture than you find on your Facebook feed. The enemy will try to offend you to keep you from reading the Word. He will tell you it is not necessary to read each day or that you already know enough of the Word to cope with life. No matter what he tells you, the truth is that life flows a whole lot more smoothly with less worry and concern when you are faithfully reading the Word for yourself each day.

Over the years, I have meditated on many scriptures, and they have become life verses to me. Certain scriptures in the Bible totally define me and my life. Knowing these passages in real life and having them as testimony will really help you. It's very powerful when you can go to the Bible and read passages that are real life prophecies over your life. Do you know that when someone gives a public prophecy, you can receive it for yourself? The same can be said about passages in the Bible that were written over the lives of other people, and as you ponder and meditate on them, you can make them your own.

Just a word on prayer. I have found that the more that you see your prayers answered, the more you make an effort to pray. If you have prayed a number of times and you have never seen an answer to prayer, you might feel like giving up on your prayer life. I was once told by Jesus as he quoted a paraphrase of James 4:2, "You have not because you ask not." It took some years and Jesus repeating that a couple of times for me to start to become a lot more active in asking for things.

As for prayer, the communication between me and Jesus, that conversation continues all the time. Each day, I am immersed in the presence of the Holy Spirit, and I am regularly talking back and forth with Jesus. I address how to have a two-way conversational prayer life with God in my book, *How to Hear God's Voice: Keys to Two-Way Conversational Prayer*. I encourage everyone to develop the ability to be able to converse back and forth with the three members of the Trinity.

Attending church is vital to a Christian and very necessary for you to grow and glean knowledge and the wisdom of God. If you are called to ministry, you need to have relationships with other Christians. Don't let offense or laziness stop you from being part of a community of believers. I have made that mistake a number of times, and it didn't go well with me when I stopped going to church. We have to grow and be whole and accept that every relationship takes some give and take. You will be offended; you will be hurt by Christians, but that is not a valid reason to quit going to church. Attending church allows you to be Christlike, not just in theory but in practice.

# LESSON 9: OLD TESTAMENT LAW VS. NEW TESTAMENT GRACE

GOD'S LAW: God gave the Ten Commandments, called the law, to expose our personal sin to us so that we would welcome a Savior.

1) God said, "You shall have no other gods before Me" (Exodus 20:3).
Question: Do YOU love God more than any other person or anything else in your life?

2) God said, "You shall not make for yourself a carved image . . ." (Exodus 20:4).
Question: Have YOU ever exalted anything before God?

3) God said, "You shall not take the name of the Lord your God in vain . . ." (Exodus 20:7).
Question: Have YOU ever used God's name as a swear word?

4) God said, "Remember the Sabbath day, to keep it holy" (Exodus 20:8).
Question: Have YOU always set aside a day each week to honor and worship God?

5) God said, "Honor your father and your mother . . ." (Exodus 20:12).
Question: Did YOU always honor your mother and father in your youth?

6) God said, "You shall not murder" (Exodus 20:13).
Question: Have YOU ever become extremely angry with a person? Murder begins in the heart. Jesus said, "Whoever is angry with his brother without cause shall

be in danger of the judgment . . . . And whoever says, 'You fool!' shall be in danger of hell fire." (Matthew 5:21b-22).

7) God said, "You shall not commit adultery" (Exodus 20:14).
<u>Question</u>: Have YOU ever looked at a woman and lusted after her? Jesus said in Matthew 5:28-30, "Whoever looks at a woman to lust for her has already committed adultery with her in his heart." Jesus goes on to say that "if your eye or your hand causes you to sin, you should pluck it out or cut it off rather than go to hell."

8) God said, "You shall not steal" (Exodus 20:15).
<u>Question</u>: Have YOU ever taken something that did not belong to you?

9) God said, "You shall not bear false witness against your neighbor" (Exodus 20:16).
<u>Question</u>: Have YOU always told the truth?

10) God said, "You shall not covet your neighbor's house; you shall not covet your neighbor's wife nor his male servant, nor his female servant, nor his ox, nor his donkey, nor anything that is your neighbor's" (Exodus 20:17).
<u>Question</u>: Have YOU ever had the desire to have what belongs to someone else?

God knew that we could never keep his law in our own strength! God knew that without the law, we would tend to judge ourselves against other people's performance. In doing so, we might believe that we are qualified for heaven.

When Jesus was on earth, he was criticized for socializing with sinners. He said, "Those who are well have no need of a physician, but those who are sick. I did not come to call the righteous, but sinners, to repentance" (Mark 2:17).

If we believe that we are righteous, then we have no need of a Savior. Yet the above test proves that we all fall way short of God's goodness. Therefore, we all need a merciful Savior, and his name is the Lord Jesus Christ.

<u>NEW TESTAMENT GRACE</u>: If Jesus had not come to earth as a Spirit-filled God-man and suffered for our sin, we wouldn't have New Testament grace.

We all need to come to terms with the fact that we have all broken the Ten Commandments. However, James 2:10 tells us that "whoever keeps the whole law and yet stumbles in one point, he is guilty of all."

God sent the law to reveal our sin to us so that we would reach out to him to save us from sin's penalty. We all need a Savior; we all need to be born-again spiritually before we die. When we honestly repent and ask the Lord Jesus Christ to come into our heart to be our Lord and Savior, we receive at that very moment God's righteousness, which justifies us in his sight.

Biblical grace means undeserved peace and favor with Father God. We need to exercise God's grace to others, knowing that, "for by grace you have been saved through faith, and that not of yourselves; it is the gift of God, not of works, lest anyone should boast" (Ephesians 2:8-9).

Most people believe that they are basically good people, but they are deceived by the devil. The Bible says, "There is a way that seems right to a man, but its end is the way of death" (Proverbs 14:12). First, the devil cleverly denies his own existence, and then he convinces people that living a so-called good life will automatically qualify them for a place in heaven.

But eternal peace with God comes from giving our lives to Jesus and responding to his gift of grace. In Christ, every believer has the same right-standing with God as Jesus Christ does, for we have been given the righteousness of God, according to 2 Corinthians 5:21. God "loves" everyone, but his delight in people varies.

My Bible notes talk about the walk of faith and say, "Jesus motivates believers to live righteously by emphasizing that such living comes from the heart through faith. Believers are already justified in God's sight, for no sin is held against them as they have responded to the grace of God on the cross."[9]

We could never repay God for what he has done for us. We can't add anything of ourselves to make us worthy of heaven. God's grace is not only receiving his power to live the Christian life, but his grace is his totally underserved goodness to us. If we could deserve forgiveness in our own strength, it would not be grace. Before we came to Christ, we were like dead people and unable to earn God's favor.

Only the Holy Spirit can convict us of sin. He hovers over an unbeliever for perhaps years, drawing them to seek answers about life, and he creates a sense of un-fulfillment within them. He also arranges for the hearing of the gospel and encourages them to respond. If God did not initiate the relationship, no one could. Of ourselves, we can't seek God because we are all born spiritually DEAD!

Dead is dead; there are no degrees of being dead! (Just like no one can be a little bit pregnant, we can't be a little bit dead.) Being spiritually dead automatically makes a person an enemy of God because that person is controlled by the devil even if he or she might seem good.

---

[9] Hayford, *The New Spirit-Filled Life Bible*.

We are all born as slaves of the devil. To be released from slavery, we need a new Master to rescue us. The blood of Jesus was the ransom price that purchased our freedom. That is why the devil hates the blood and why Christians glory in the blood of Jesus. We could not free ourselves from sin; only the perfect God-man Jesus Christ could do that for us, and he did.

Jesus said that no one is good except God (See Luke 18:19). I can't boast and tell others that I am good, but I can and DO say to the devil, "All the righteousness of Christ Jesus dwells in me." That's true!

Read Ephesians 2:4-9. Being "good" is not mentioned. To be rescued from God's judgment for sin, we need to have a relationship with him. We need his grace to work in our lives. This passage lists five reasons for salvation, and they have all been done by God through Jesus Christ himself.

- God's mercy and love is spoken of in verse 4.
- God makes a spiritually dead person become spiritually alive (v. 5).
- God sees Christians alive in him here on earth and heaven at the same time (v. 6).
- God's kindness toward his children (v. 7).
- God's grace is spoken of in verses 5, 7, and 8. God's grace alone saves us.

The parable of the Pharisee and the tax collector is recorded in Luke 18:9-14. The following thoughts are taken from the book, _The Complete Discipleship Evangelism Course_ by Don Krow. Let's read the parable.

"Also He spoke this parable to some who trusted in themselves that they were righteous, and despised others: Two men went up to the temple to pray, one a Pharisee and the other a tax collector" (verses 9-10).

Pharisees thought that, because they were religious leaders of Old Testament studies, they were far more honorable than the common man. On the other hand, tax collectors were known to be sinful, for they often collected taxes by any means they could. They gave some of the money to the Roman government but kept a sizable portion for themselves. A tax collector was not respected by anyone.

"The Pharisee stood and prayed thus with himself, 'God, I thank You that I am not like other men – extortionists, unjust, adulterers, even as this tax collector. I fast twice a week. I give tithes of all that I possess'" (verses 11-12).

Note: The Pharisee prayed "thus with himself." He went on to boast, "God, I thank you that I am not like other men." He meant that he was not sinful like the tax collector standing close by.

The tax collector was actually standing "afar off." He was ashamed to go into the temple. He knew he was a terrible sinner, so he remained outside. He wouldn't even lift his eyes to heaven. He just acknowledged his own sin and cried out, "God be merciful to me; I am a sinner!" (verse 13b).

"Jesus said, 'I tell you, this man went down to his house justified rather than the other, for everyone who exalts himself will be humbled, and he who humbles himself will be exalted'" (verse 14).

Grace is only offered to those who humble themselves and who cry out for God's mercy. These people will find both mercy and pardon from God.

Proud people look down on others. This Pharisee was full of pride; he didn't think HE needed a Savior. "If we say that we have no sin, we deceive ourselves, and the truth is not in us. If we confess our sins, He is faithful and just to forgive us our sins and to cleanse us from all unrighteousness" (1 John 1:8-9).[10]

SUMMARY: Trying to live under the law actually strengthens our sin nature as the law entices us to sin. For example, if you saw a sign near a wall that said, "Wet Paint—Don't Touch," what would be your immediate reaction?

I know that I would probably lightly touch it just to see for myself if it was still wet.

If I hadn't seen the sign, I wouldn't have thought about touching the wall, but when told not to do it, I would be enticed to do it! God knows this about the human heart. "The sting of death is sin, and the strength of sin is the law. But thanks be to God, who gives us the victory through our Lord Jesus Christ" (1 Corinthians 15:56-57).

Regardless of personal sins, we are all on a level playing field. In God's sight, Mother Teresa needed salvation just as much as Hitler did. We were born with a sin nature; we all need a Savior. His name is Jesus, and he is the only person who has been appointed and fully approved of, by Father God.

- If animal sacrifices in the Old Testament could make people perfect, there would have been no need to repeat them year after year.
- Old Testament sacrifices were part of the law. They temporarily covered sin, but they couldn't remove sin's guilt.
- Only belief in the Lord Jesus Christ and the power of the Holy Spirit can break the power of sin.
- Any type of religious thinking makes us sin conscous instead of Christ-focused. Believers can only boast in what God has done for them.

---

[10] Andrew Wommack and Don Krow, *The Complete Discipleship Evangelism Course: Condensed Version and Workbook*.

Once we are saved, good works done by the power of the Holy Spirit living in us will and should flow from us. These are a good witness to others of the power of God in our lives.

NOTE: The chart I used at the start of this lesson was adapted from a book by Don Krow and Andrew Wommack called, *The Complete Discipleship Evangelism Course: Condensed Version and Workbook*. (Their book is to be used for discipleship purposes only and is not to be used for financial gain.)

In this book, Don Krow challenges a friend whether he would make it to heaven. I listed the Ten Commandments taken directly from my Bible in Exodus 20. Then, I used some of Don's discussion with his friend to make up the chart at the beginning of this lesson.

For by grace you have been saved through faith, and that not of yourselves; it is the gift of God, not of works, lest anyone should boast (Ephesians 2:8-9).

**Matthew's Comments**
It does not matter how long you have been saved and walking with Jesus, whenever you read the Ten Commandments, they seem to pull you up short if you are honest with yourself. I know as I read them along with my mother's questions, I was convicted of where I fail.

That is why the gospel is good news—better news than we can even fathom. The fact that Jesus's death and blood saved us and washed us clean from sin once and for all is simply better news than we actually deserve.

And that is the reason it is called grace. It is favor that I did not deserve, unmerited favor given to me. When I am honest with myself, I tend to fall short of perfection all the time. Through the reading of this chapter, I have come to realize just what a great work Jesus did coming to earth.

Were you convicted as you read the law and as you read my mother's questions? Do you feel that you have in fallen short in some way? If you did feel convicted too, you can thank God for his mercy in your life and that he made a way for you to be cleansed and righteous in his sight.

# LESSON 10: GOD WANTS TO FINANCIALLY BLESS US

"Beloved, I pray that you may prosper in all things and be in health, just as your soul prospers" (3 John 1:2). God wants us to be well and to prosper in all things so that we can be a financial blessing to others.

AUTHOR'S TESTIMONY: Before we came to Coffs Harbour in January 1976, Bob had a senior position in the Sydney Mail Exchange Sorting Office with excellent pay. He worked lots of overtime with great compensation. One day, he was offered a blue-collar job by his brother-in-law in Coffs Harbour. He was thrilled about it as he was fed up with all the in-fighting at his government workplace.

As the bookkeeper of our family, I saw two major problems. First, our income would be halved, and we were not tithing, so I believed that God's financial blessing would not be on us. I shared this with Bob, and he agreed to tithe. Within weeks, he recommitted his life to Jesus. Since that time, God has really blessed our marriage and has provided for all our needs.

Today, forty-two years later, we are in our late seventies and receive an Age Pension from the government, yet tithing is still a pleasure. God has proved to us again and again that we can never out-give him. In addition, trusting God with our finances gives us confidence that we can trust him in other matters as well. In fact, tithing gives a peace that money can't buy. Not only that, God has used us to be a financial blessing to others who are struggling, which thrills our hearts.

Andrew Wommack has subtitled his book, *Financial Stewardship*, with this phrase: *Experiencing the Freedom of Turning Your Finances Over to God*. As the subject of my book is on discipleship, I have composed a separate list of his conclusions regarding our finances.

God is the source of all good things, and when he knows we trust him with our money, he will open the windows of heaven and pour out his blessings onto us and our families. (See Malachi 3:10-11.) Genuine wisdom about money begins by tithing. *One-tenth of our income should be given to the place we are spiritually fed each week.* Offerings given to other worthy causes are secondary to our tithe; they should not replace our local church tithe. "The generous soul will be made rich and he who waters will also be watered himself" (Proverbs 11:25).

A good steward is wise with their money and trusts God with their finances.

Knowing that God is the source of everything good gives us the assurance that whatever happens, we will be okay financially. Actually, everything that we have earned, inherited, or given to us by others has really come from God.

Don't see your ten percent love gift as a burden; rather, see the 90 percent that we keep as God's gift to us. After all, God gave us the health, the ability, and the opportunity to have money in the first place. Trusting God in the area of finances helps us to trust him with other more important issues, like salvation or physical healing for our loved ones.

We are told in 1 Peter 4:10 to be "good stewards of the manifold grace of God." Without God's grace, we wouldn't be able to earn money, so changing our mindset from "owner" to "steward" makes tithing easier. Instead of money controlling us, it becomes a tool to use for God's glory.

As Christians, we inherited the blessings of Abraham as part of our new-birth experience. This includes spiritual, emotional, physical, and material blessings. God is the one who opens doors of opportunity for us. One name for God is *El Shaddai*, which means "I am the God who pours out blessings, who gives abundantly and continually."[11]

Long before Jesus came to earth, God required the Jewish people to make regular sacrifices to him, and his complaint to them was always directed to their heart attitude in doing so.

God didn't need those animal sacrifices, but he was trying to illustrate the need for innocent blood to be spilled so that future generations could be made righteous. You see, the sacrificial offerings back then foreshadowed how Christ would ultimately offer his own blood as payment for our sins.

Blood sacrifices in Old Testament times were a shadow of the future death of Christ on the cross. The Old Testament animal sacrifices were not for God's benefit but for the benefit of his people. The Jews were going through the motions of making their offerings, but their hearts were far from God.

Tithing basically comes down to our faith in God's goodness!

When we tithe, God knows that we really trust in his goodness. "You shall remember the Lord your God, for it is He who gives you power to get wealth" (Deuteronomy 8:18a). Put his goodness to the test and begin to tithe.

Seeing our role as a steward of God's resources will save us from experiencing financial stress. A steward knows that his master wouldn't want him to go into debt and pay lots of interest unless it was absolutely essential. Yes, people can prosper without God's intervention, but it often comes with heartache. But "the blessing of the Lord makes one rich, and He adds no sorrow with it" (Proverbs 10:22).

---

[11] "Genesis 17 – God Reaffirms the Covenant," Enduring Word, David Guzak, accessed February 5, 2018, https://enduringword.com/bible-commentary/genesis-17/

By personally managing our finances, we carry the load of responsibility. God, however, wants us to seek his blessings, and he will supply our physical needs. Jesus said, "Seek first the kingdom of God and His righteousness, and all these things shall be added to you" (Matthew 6:33). God is good; he is never stingy or forgetful about his promises to us.

Prosperity comes from seeing God as our source of supply with the mindset of being a steward. Once we adopt these two principles, God will cause us to prosper. In the story in Matthew 14:16:21 about the five loaves and the two fish, we learn that God is a skilled multiplier, and he just wants to bless us so that we can be a greater blessing to others. God doesn't need our money, but he wants us to exercise our faith in his goodness to us.

Jesus said, "He who is faithful in what is least is faithful also in much; and he who is unjust in what is least is unjust also in much" (Luke 16:10). Trusting God with our finances is the starting point of exercising faith. We probably won't really be able to trust God for big things until we can first trust him with money.

When the rich young ruler asked Jesus how he could receive eternal life, Jesus, knowing the man's heart, replied, "You still lack one thing. Sell all that you have and distribute to the poor, and you will have treasure in heaven; and come, follow me" (Luke 18:22). Jesus was saying, "If you can't trust me in that which is least, (money) then you won't be able to trust me for that which is greater."

Money is nothing compared to good health or healthy relationships. God's promise of prosperity is part of our salvation. "For you know the grace of our Lord Jesus Christ, that though He was rich, yet for your sakes He became poor, that you through His poverty might become rich" (2 Corinthians 8:9).

Jesus said that we can't serve two masters. We can't trust ourselves in money matters and then try to trust God with everything else. The same God who promised eternal life, also said in Luke 6:38, to "give" and it would be "bountifully" given back to you. When we trust God for the visible things" like money, we will be able to fully trust Him for "unseen" things like health, peace, joy, prosperity, and God's favor in our life.

God's plans for us are far bigger than our dreams. "For I know the thoughts that I think toward you, says the Lord, thoughts of peace and not of evil, to give you a future and a hope" (Jeremiah 29:11).

"Eye has not seen, nor ear heard, nor have entered into the heart of man the things which God has prepared for those who love Him" (1 Corinthians 2:9).

Become a faithful steward of God's resources as he has a great bookkeeping principle. He wants us to prosper in all things so that we can be a witness of his goodness to others. Money has power, but God has far more power.

Jesus said, "Do not lay up for yourselves treasures on earth, where moth and rust destroy and where thieves break in and steal; but lay up for yourselves treasures in heaven, where neither moth nor rust destroys and where thieves do not break in and steal. For where your treasure is, there your heart will be also" (Matthew 6:19-21). Jesus also said, "You cannot serve God and mammon" (Matthew 6:24). (Mammon is money.)

God has always blessed his faithful servants. Abraham, Isaac, King David, and his son, King Solomon, had one thing in common. They were all very prosperous because they honored God with their money. *They learned that trusting God in all other matters starts with finances!*

If we think, "I want to give, but I can't, I need this money," this means our confidence or reliance is on our own source of supply. In 2 Corinthians 5:17, believers are called a new creation. Therefore as a new creation, old mindsets like doubting must change.

Read the parable of the "unjust steward" in Luke 16:1-13. Expecting to get-rich-quick is not part of God's plan for us. This steward wanted to steal money, inherit it, or come by it effortlessly somehow. He knew that he was going to be sacked, but he was too proud to beg and too lazy to work, so he kept on stealing. But he was very shrewd. Instead of putting his employer's money into his own pocket, he invested in other people who *owed his master money,* knowing that he was building a safety net for his future.

Then, when he lost his job, he planned to go to the master's debtors and say, "Can you give me a hand as I have lost my job?" They would feel indebted to him because he had saved them so much money. He could "mooch" off them instead of getting a job.

The master's response, however, was surprising, for in Luke 16:8, we read, "So the master commended the unjust steward, because he had dealt shrewdly. For the sons of this world are more shrewd in their generation than the sons of light." This unusual response says a lot about the master's attitude toward his money because he didn't get angry or demand justice!

His master must have already learned that money was just a tool to use; it was the byproduct of the favor of God on his life. We too are to learn that God is the source of our wealth, much like the story of the goose that lays golden eggs. The golden eggs were not as valuable as the goose that produced them. In a similar way, genuine treasure is the blessings and the favor of God.

Once we realize that God is the source of prosperity, we see how pointless it is to chase riches. God told the Jewish people, "And you shall remember the Lord your God, for it is He who gives you power to get wealth, that He may establish His covenant which He swore to your fathers, as it is this day" (Deuteronomy 8:18).

God releases an anointing on certain things we do. He causes us to prosper, and his blessings are so powerful that they can't be reversed. In fact, the only thing that can derail the blessing of God is our own unbelief and negativity. When we can look at all our possessions and genuinely say, "It's just stuff," we have learned that money is only a tool that helps us accomplish God-given goals. This master had such a godly understanding of wealth that he could even compliment a thief.

A financial crisis might push some people over the edge, but if we are like this master, we won't be shaken, for our trust is in the Lord. The true power of money is in using it to change our future.

The problem with the unjust servant was that he tried to use his master's money to bring change to his own future. Yet Jesus said the master praised the steward. Yes, he was using his master's money to bribe people, but his master recognized that at least he was preparing for his own future. The master wasn't commending the steward for the act of stealing; *he was complimenting him for finally figuring out that money is a tool that could affect his future.*

As Christians, we can touch people's lives through giving, and after we die, those people will be lined up in heaven to thank us for the way we used our resources to help them. This is storing up treasure in heaven. Jesus said, "Make friends for yourselves by unrighteous mammon, that when you fail they may receive you into an everlasting home" (Luke 16:9). In the Greek, this word fail can also mean death or die. The unrighteous mammon is, of course, money.

There's no money in heaven. But by investing money into the lives of others, you can take something destined for destruction and turn it into something eternal. Additionally, by investing money into gospel outreaches, you will be touching lives of total strangers for whom Jesus died for.

Sadly, some Christians will not have much treasure stored up in heaven because they only used their money for selfish reasons.

God wants us to live in comfort, dress well, and own nice things. He doesn't want us to be poor. He is not against us taking care of ourselves. But he knows that our attitude toward many things will change when we really have a revelation on the proper meaning of prosperity.

We are to understand that a man is not a fool to give away something he can't keep in order to get something he can never lose. Know that God is always in the people business. Material things will fade away, and the only thing that will matter in eternity is how much we have invested into the lives of other people.

In the meantime, we are to keep a balance between planning for the future and living in the moment. The blessing of God is what makes us rich, not money. As long as you have God's blessing, wealth will find you! The key is learning not to spend all of your money on short-lived pleasures but to use some of it to help shape your future. Money is not just for spending on earth now but so that multitudes of people will be waiting to welcome you into heaven.

When the master told the steward he would be fired, the steward finally realized that he had better plan for his future. He took the money he had access to and used the influence and power it gave him to prepare his future. Though he did it dishonestly, the fact is, we need to also prepare for our future in heaven. When we get there, we will want more than anything else to see and meet all the people we have invested our money in by helping financially in gospel outreach. Then we will hear the Lord say to us, *"Well done my good and faithful servant."* Those words from Jesus on that day will thrill us more than anything else we have ever experienced. In the meantime, we are to keep a balance between planning for the future and living in the moment.

Apart from my personal testimony, this lesson has mostly come from my very condensed version of the first four chapters of Andrew's book, *Financial Stewardship*. His Spirit-filled teaching on many subjects has changed my Christian life. For nearly thirty years, I was a legalistic born-again believer, but in 2005, my son

Matthew played a CD on Andrew's teaching on law and grace, and I was set free from legalism.

I encourage you, my reader, to view money as God wants you to. I have included a separate summary sheet with brief comments from Andrew taken from every chapter of his book on financial stewardship. Enjoy.

### ANDREW'S SHORT PROVERBS ON MONEY

- Money is meant to be your servant not a master that rules over you.
- One of the reasons we don't see greater prosperity in our lives is that we haven't learned the lesson of being a steward.
- Seeing yourself as a steward brings peace of mind and a sense of security.
- Jesus said that money is the area of trusting God in the least of things.
- Using your faith for finances is the smallest use of faith, and if you haven't done that which is least, then you won't be able to do greater things.
- One reason so many Christians are stuck in their walk with the Lord is that they haven't started trusting God in the area of finances.
- God doesn't ask for tithes and offerings because he needs your money. He asks because he wants you to learn to trust him with all your heart, and finances are the first step in that direction.
- Once you begin trusting God for that which is seen—money—then you will be able to trust him for that which is unseen: health, peace, joy, prosperity, and God's favor in your life.
- The blessing and favor of God—not money—are what make you rich.

- The true power of money is in using it to change your future.
- A man is not a fool to give away something he can't keep in order to get something he can never lose.
- Prosperity is a byproduct, not the goal, of seeking God.
- Prosperity isn't about you; it's really about how much money is flowing *through* you.
- God assumes the responsibility of taking care of you when you put seeking his kingdom first. And God can take better care of you than you can of yourself.
- The motive behind what you do is more important than the action itself.
- Prosperity is having enough so that you can abound unto every good work.
- If God can get money through you, he'll get it to you, and it won't be long before you have plenty left over for yourself.
- You are not under a curse if you don't tithe.
- We don't tithe to please God; we do it out of a sense of appreciation for all that God has done for us.
- God loves a cheerful giver.
- Where you give your money is important.
- Your return is going to depend to a degree on how fruitful the ground is where you are sowing.
- Taking 10 percent of what you make and giving it away makes no sense to the natural mind, which is exactly why God asks us to do it!
- Giving is really about trusting God and acting on your faith.
- You not only reap what you sow, you reap the way you sow.

**Matthew's Comments**

I don't live in the United States, but I hear reports about prosperity preachers there and the work of TV evangelists who try to appeal to people to give to them and their ministries. Understandably, many Christians have been totally put off about the subject of money because of these ministries that try to fleece the flock. A measure of truth lies in what they teach, and as you have read what my mother has said and what Andrew Wommack has said, you might have started to reconsider your stance when it comes to money.

A few years ago, I started my book-publishing ministry and started to provide prophecies for people and other services for a donation. The Lord has seen fit to bless me, and I have never had a book that was ready to be published without the money to do it. This is a big deal as each book costs me about two thousand dollars AUD to copy edit, have a cover designed, and to publish. I have been faithful with my giving to the Lord, and he has been faithful to provide the finances that I have needed. I personally sow about 30 percent of my income each week to the Lord.

It takes a real shift in your mind to tithe and give to God. So many people suffer from a poverty mindset and a fear of lack. It really takes faith to step out and start to give to God. But I do encourage you to step out and start to tithe and give to God. Later when you are used to doing it, you will be very pleased that you started. I like to say tithing to a Christian is putting your money where your mouth is!

The best book that I ever read on giving was *Financial Stewardship* by Andrew Wommack, and I trust that you might spend the money to purchase it and learn from it.

# LESSON 11: LET YOUR LIGHT SHINE!

Whenever we blend in with the ways of the world, others will not see Jesus in us. He said, "You are the light of the world . . . . Let your light so shine before men, that they may see your good works and glorify your Father in heaven" (Matthew 5:14a, 16).

After his resurrection, Jesus said to his disciples "Peace to you! As the Father has sent Me, I also send you" (John 20:21). God told us to make disciples for him and to be his representatives on earth, for he wants to enlarge his family.

Once we were unknowingly separated from God and headed for hell. Then, because someone loved us and regularly prayed for us, the Holy Spirit began to draw us to God and now we are part of his big family. Our task is to demonstrate and to share our faith with others so that they too can come to know God. Believers worldwide are to be God's ministers of reconciliation. (See 2 Corinthians 5:18.) To put it simply, we are to share and to demonstrate the love of Jesus with others so that they too will come to salvation.

Most people are on the wide path to hell as we once were (Matthew 7:13-14). The narrow path has only a few on it but leads to eternal life. Only Jesus can transfer us to the path leading to heaven. He said in John 14:6, "I am the way, the truth and the life. No one comes to the Father except through Me." The Apostle Paul said of Jesus, "There is no other name under heaven given among men by whom we must be saved" (Acts 4:12).

God wants all Christians to share their faith in Jesus with others. Ask God for his wisdom and boldness to do this. We are simply called to sow seeds of faith, for it is only the Holy Spirit who can convict a person of sin. You might be the only Christian or the only living Bible that some people will ever know.

Our everyday words and actions to others already witness much about the real us so let it be a good witness. Jesus said, "By this My Father is glorified, that you bear much fruit; so you will be My disciples" (John 15:8). If you have been born again, this fruit is the nine fruit of the Holy Spirit already within you: love, joy, peace, patience, kindness, goodness, faithfulness, gentleness and self-control. (See Galatians 5:22-23.)

Other tangible good fruit are new Christians who have come to the Lord due to your love and prayers for them. Good fruit will also result when a believer takes the time to lovingly help people in their day-to-day struggles. Our Lord constantly helped others.

Once, a man blind from birth received his sight from Jesus. He was confronted by the angry religious leaders, so he simply said in John 9:25b, "One thing I know; once I was blind, now I see." Isn't that our story too? Once we were *spiritually blind*, but now we see! This man didn't know the gospel message; he only knew that Jesus had miraculously given him sight.

But we must know that, regardless of how well the Gospel is presented or demonstrated, only the Holy Spirit can break through human unbelief, for salvation is always a work of God, not man.

We are to pray for unbelievers and be Christ in visible form to them. (Knowledge about God's love won't bring salvation unless the Holy Spirit has first softened a person's heart.)

People lack true spiritual knowledge; they don't know that they are on the wrong path and that there is a far better path. Freedom to choose is the responsibility and the privilege that God has given to us all. Personal choice is the most extravagant gift we have ever received because it cost Father God his Son!

To be a witness for Jesus, it's helpful to have a salvation plan in mind. Let's look at four verses in the book of Romans. Highlight them in yellow so that you can easily find them.

1. Find Romans 3:23. Next to it, write Romans 6:23.
2. Next to Romans 6:23, write Romans 5:8.
3. Next to Romans 5:8, write in Romans 10:13.
4. Romans 10:13 is the final verse. You are now equipped to briefly explain the Gospel.

Ask an unbeliever the following questions and show them the verses from your Bible.

1. Romans 3:23 - At birth, what was our spiritual condition?
2. Romans 6:23 - What is the result of sin?
3. Romans 5:8 - What has God done about our sin?
4. Romans 10:13 - How does anyone receive God's salvation?

As Christians, we know that Jesus has forgiven our sin and has promised us eternal life in heaven. His Holy Spirit, in us gives us the peace and guarantee that we are different from before our salvation. Therefore, because we have firsthand experience of salvation, we can share our testimony with others, including:

1. Our own personal story, which is our testimony of our life before salvation.
2. The circumstances of how we were saved.
3. Our life since our salvation.

After the crucifixion, we read in Acts 3:1-10 that a man who was lame from birth sat at the gate leading to the Jewish temple and begged for money. People gave him some spare coins. One day Peter and John, who were full of faith in the power of Jesus's name, came up to this man. Peter said, "Silver and gold I do not have, but what I do have I give you; "In the name of Jesus Christ of Nazareth, rise up and walk." Peter then helped the man to his feet, and the happy man went into the temple, walking and leaping and praising God!

My Bible notes on Acts 3:16 say, "After the Spirit's outpouring at Pentecost, many wonders and signs were done through the apostles."[12] Peter attributed this healing to no human power but to the mighty saving faith in the precious name of Jesus!

In a courtroom today, a witness isn't expected to argue the case, prove the truth, or press for a verdict because that's the job of the lawyers. Witnesses simply report what happened or what they saw! That is exactly what this former lame man did when he was confronted with questions.

The risen Lord Jesus said in Acts 1:8, "You will be my witnesses." Believers need to share their testimony with others and to share Bible truth as we know it. We will never know everything about God in this lifetime. But God uses our words to help someone else. Sharing the gospel is like one beggar telling another beggar where to find some food. Therefore, telling others about Jesus is a very loving thing to do.

That's why personal testimony stories are so great; we are the ONLY authority on our life. Therefore, it's impossible for others to argue about our personal experience. But we must be prepared to pay the price for giving our testimony, for the devil hates us doing this. He will try to tell us that our life is not impressive enough for us to share our stories.

Remember, our testimony is not just about what *we* have done. The power of our testimony is all about what God has done for us! That's why we will have an *ongoing* testimony to share.

A testimony is more powerful to an unbeliever than a polished sermon because we are the only authority on our life. Others will see us as being a satisfied customer of Jesus. Don't allow the devil to place the fear of man onto you. Know that when we share what Jesus has done in our life, we do two great things:

1. We give glory to God for his work of saving us.

---

[12] Hayford, *The New Spirit-Filled Life Bible*.

2. We give others the chance to come to know God's love and salvation for themselves.

List some names of unbelievers that you know and love. Then, ask God to place spiritually mature Christian friends into their life. Ask him also to give you his love for these people and to give you an open opportunity to witness to them. Pray against the particular obstacles they might have in their lives, such as:

- Ignorance: Some people simply don't know the gospel message. Once, we were all like that. Pray for the Holy Spirit's intervention and for God's timing and for your boldness to share the Gospel. *But most of all, be like Christ to them.*

- Resentment: Some people blame God for the suffering in the world, so they don't want to know him. Lovingly share with them points from Lesson 12 on evil and suffering. *But most of all, be like Christ to them.*

- Wrong belief systems: Some people have occult beliefs, such as astrology, horoscope reading, fortune telling, clairvoyance, and similar beliefs. Some people might be of other faiths. In Jesus's name, pray against Satan's lies and pray that they will come to the knowledge of the one true God. *But most of all, be like Christ to them.*

- Hurt people: Some people might have been deeply hurt by other church attenders. Pray that the Holy Spirit will draw mature Christians into their lives, and they will come to know Jesus as Lord of their life. Perhaps God has called you to be that person. *But most of all, be like Christ to them.*

- Worldly people: Some people might be materialistic; money, possessions, a career, or a hobby might be their god. In Jesus's name, pray against the strongholds that Satan has placed in their lives and that God will create a need that money, power, fame, or nothing else can fill. Pray also against the spirit of unbelief. *But most of all, be like Christ to them.*

- Good works: Most people believe that their good works will get them to heaven. In Jesus's name, pray against the religious spirit that is lying to them. Pray that the Holy Spirit will soften their hearts to hear and to respond to the gospel. *But most of all, be like Christ to them.*

Always remember to pray against the powers of darkness in the authority of Jesus's name and in the power of his blood. Otherwise, demons might try to cause trouble for you or your loved ones.

I believe that every Christian had someone praying for them long before they were saved. You can be that praying person for someone. The Bible teaches that God knew those who would receive him long before he laid the foundations of the world. (See Ephesians1:4-5 and 2:10.)

A Christian neighbor befriended me; she patiently helped me with my son, and she invited me to a function where I would hear the gospel for the first time. I was saved that July day in 1972 and have remained strong in the Lord because Jesus is the best friend anyone could have.

A continual spiritual battle is being fought around us all (Ephesians 6:12). The kingdom of Satan constantly opposes the Kingdom of God. Satan wants to deceive everyone because God loves all his creation and gave up his own life for all humanity.

The battle between good and evil is real. Because of the ignorance of many people, evil is claiming ground at an alarming rate today. Many things in the world are extremely frightening, and the Bible says that things will get worse, not better. Then at the appointed time, the Lord Jesus Christ will return as king and judge.

It is not God's will that anyone should be lost. "The Lord is not slack concerning His promise, as some count slackness, but is longsuffering toward us, not willing that any should perish, but that all should come to repentance" (2 Peter 3:9). God wants everyone to respond to his love.

"Who desires all men to be saved and to come to the knowledge of the truth. For there is one God and one Mediator between God and men, the Man Christ Jesus, who gave Himself a ransom for all" (1Timothy 2:4-5). Our triune God is the giver of salvation.

"Quietly trust yourself to Christ your Lord and if anybody asks why you believe as you do, be ready to tell him, and do it in a gentle and respectful way" (1 Peter 3:15, The Living Bible).

You might not always have a Bible handy, so practice verbalizing the brief Romans gospel message in this lesson. Practice until you feel confident about sharing it. Most importantly, ask the Holy Spirit to lead you and to give you his wisdom and love for the particular person you seek to see saved.

Jesus was the perfect example of genuine humility.

"Let this mind be in you which was also in Christ Jesus, who, being in the form of God, did not consider it robbery to be equal with God, but made Himself of no reputation, taking the form of a bondservant, and coming in the likeness of men. And being found in appearance as a man, He humbled Himself and became obedient to the point of death, even the death of the cross.

"Therefore God also has highly exalted Him and given Him the name which is above every name, that at the name of Jesus every knee should bow, of those in heaven, and of those on earth, and of those under the earth, and that every tongue should confess that Jesus Christ is Lord, to the glory of God the Father" (Philippians 2:5-11).

One day, all people, both the resurrected dead plus all the living people on earth, will bow to the Lord Jesus Christ, but it will be too late for the unbelieving dead or the unbelieving living to repent on that day. The gates of heaven will be closed to them!

"Behold, now is the accepted time; behold, now is the day of salvation" (2 Corinthians 6:2b).

**Matthew's Comments**

Our lives should become a living Bible for people to read. Many people who don't know Jesus won't pick up a Bible one day and say to themselves, "I want to know what Christians believe." Some might, but the majority of unbelievers read the lives of the Christians that they know. If you are known as a Christian, you can be sure that people are watching you and trying to work out if your faith is worthwhile and authentic.

From time to time as the Holy Spirit leads them, people might ask you about your faith. This is not the time to be scared or nervous as you can be sure that the Holy Spirit is leading them to ask the question in the first place. Take the time to tell them stories of how Jesus has made a difference in your life. Simply relax and share some good stories with them, stories that show that Jesus is alive and willing to be a part of their lives also.

I had a brother who never used to go to church or share his faith with anyone. He believed the lie that his life was not a strong enough example of the Christian faith for him to witness for Jesus. He had a roommate that was always watching documentaries on evolution who made fun of my brother's faith. One day, my brother had enough and told the roommate to watch a series of documentaries about creation that showed the obvious flaws in Darwin's theory of evolution. The roommate then asked my brother how he could become a Christian. If you had asked me if my brother would be able to lead anyone to the Lord, I would have said that I didn't think so. But God in his wisdom had better ideas.

The point of that story is that every one of us has a story and tools that can help us lead others to the Lord. My brother had been watching the movies on creation for his own interest with no desire to show them to anyone else. Yet at the right time, the Holy Spirit led him to show them to his roommate, and the Holy Spirit convicted his friend. You also can be a witness for Jesus.

# LESSON 12: WHY DO BAD THINGS HAPPEN TO GOOD PEOPLE?

Perhaps like most people, you have contemplated, "What is God doing about evil and suffering?"

This question needs to be answered because Satan uses this topic to discredit God's goodness.

Therefore, we need to understand that there are some things that God can't do, such as sin or go back on his Word. Furthermore, he cannot always stop pain and suffering from happening.

Way back in the Garden of Eden, God gave Adam and Eve a free will, which ultimately led them and all future generations into trouble. Even today, all of us make individual choices that cause us heartache. People of the world will experience heartache more often because they do not have God's Holy Spirit influencing their decision making.

Therefore, we can rightly say that, ever since Adam and Eve disobeyed God in the Garden of Eden, mankind in general is a race of fallen people. Even at the moment of birth, we have the capacity to sin, for we all inherited Adam's sin nature within our human soul. Therefore, unconsciously at times, we set ourselves up in rebellion and self-dependence. This attitude in itself has released forces of chaos, evil, and pain into our world, and even nature and creation itself has been affected by original sin.

Believers have committed themselves to God, and yes, God is in control of their lives, for he has saved them and will guide them and look after them. But believers can be gullible to Satan's lies and accusations at times. If we don't give our lives to the lordship of Jesus Christ, Satan can easily influence our thought life and the decisions we make.

As such, unbelievers are very easily deceived by Satan, for instead of God the Holy Spirit living in them, Satan, who is now legitimately, the god of this world, has control over their lives. "The gospel message is veiled . . . to those who are perishing" (2 Corinthians 4:3).

Also, we read: "For the message of the cross is foolishness to those who are perishing, but to us who are being saved it is the power of God" (1 Corinthians 1:18).

The Bible says: "Let no one deceive himself. If anyone among you seems to be wise in this age, let him become a fool that he may become wise. For the wisdom of this world is foolishness with God (1 Corinthians 3:18-19). For God "catches the wise in their own craftiness" (Job 5:13).

Man's nature was badly affected by original sin but so was creation itself. For example, an unbeliever might argue that earthquakes are just a force of nature; they have nothing to do with God. Yet we must realize that in the way that God created all things, he made a deep and profound connection between all of creation with humanity as its pinnacle.

Therefore, when sin came into the world through Adam and Eve's disobedience, it didn't just affect us, but it affected all creation because of this deep connection between us and nature.

God had given Adam and Eve the authority to rule earth and have dominion over all creation. But they lost their dominion to rule when they listened to Satan, disguised as a serpent. Not only that, but they spiritually died, for God withdrew His Holy Spirit from their soul.

Adam and Eve didn't physically die, but their human spirit was now disconnected from God. Therefore by default, Adam passed his God-given authority to rule and have dominion over to the devil. Ever since then, Satan has been the legal god of this world. Today, Satan still blinds unbelievers "lest the light of the gospel of the glory of Christ, who is the image of God, should shine on them" (2 Corinthians 4:4).

We must realize that when major natural calamities happen, it's because creation was marred at a deep structural level by man's rebellion against God.

Satan delights in every form of chaos because God is a God of order and beauty. Man's rebellion has had an on-going effect on all of us today. Until Jesus comes again to physically rule on earth, this exchange of authority from Adam to Satan has affected everything.

When God originally created earth, he set all sorts of physical laws in motion. Today, these laws remain essentially true. Some of these unchangeable laws include the law of gravity and the law of aerodynamics, helpful laws. But the law of sin and decay brings destruction, which is why earthquakes, mudslides, and all types of disasters occur.

Romans 8:20-23 talks about the earth groaning in bondage, waiting to be set free.

So how was God going to fix this problem? He could do just one of two things: he could judge rebellion, or he could heal it. If he had chosen the judging option, how many people would have been left to reproduce? None!

My Bible notes say, "The whole created universe has suffered the consequences of human sin, being subjected to decomposition, futility, and corruption. However, that process of deterioration is only temporary, because God has provided hope of deliverance. At the time of our final redemption, (Romans 8:21) creation itself will be set free from 'enslavement to decay' and will share our glory."[13]

---

[13] Hayford, *The New Spirit-Filled Life Bible*.

We have *all* rebelled against God because we have *all* inherited sin from Adam's gene pool. Judging would be a quick but not very effective fix for us or for God.

Instead, God decided to heal our rebellion. He left heaven and became a man and died for what Adam had done. People think that God is up in heaven, totally removed and distant from our pain. We might even shake our fist at him and yell, "Where are you? Don't you care? Why don't you intervene? You don't understand our pain!"

We are ignorant, or we forget that Jesus left heaven, was veiled in human flesh, and unlike us, he lived a poor man's life as an itinerate teacher. He never had a home of his own or spare money. He walked everywhere and had no material possessions other than what he wore or carried. He spent his time healing people and ministering the grace of God to all he met.

For that, he was betrayed by a close friend, arrested, tried, and convicted in an unjust court in the early hours of the morning on a trumped-up, erroneous charge. He was tortured by the most hideous process imaginable for six excruciating hours. Finally, he offered up his Spirit to his Father and died.

Isaiah 50:5-6 says, "The Lord has opened My ear; and I was not rebellious, nor did I turn away. I gave My back to those who struck Me, and My cheeks to those who plucked out the beard; I did not hide My face from shame and spitting."

The devil will whisper to you that "God doesn't care about your suffering." Instead of letting self-pity rule, read Isaiah Chapter 53. You will realize how intense the suffering of Jesus was when he gave his life for us. Prior to the cross, Jesus suffered more than we could possibly imagine. Then on the cross, he suffered the pain and isolation of the collective sin and sickness of the whole world for all time.

Yes, Jesus is well acquainted with pain and suffering.

People he grew up with rejected him, his disciples deserted him, and to top it off, on the cross, he had to experience separation from his Father in heaven for the first time ever. This was necessary because Jesus needed to completely identify with every unbeliever for all time so that they could come into a relationship with his Father through his death for them.

God was the only one who was sinless, so he was the only one who could take on someone else's sin. He did it all for us! You see, the penalty for our sin is separation from God. He loved us too much to be separated from us forever.

To God, evil and suffering is not just a rhetorical question.

He has deeply experienced it. He has actually taken evil and rebellion upon himself and taken our sin and sickness upon himself so that he could finally and irrevocably deal with them.

But you might still ask, "Where was he when I was suffering?" This is a hard question, but Jesus, through his experience on earth, can walk with you through your suffering as someone who truly knows and understands your pain.

THE RESURRECTION FACTOR: When Jesus rose from the dead, evil had thrown everything it had at him. It's like Jesus was saying to evil, "Go on, give me everything you've got! Give me your best shot!" And then he died, and God then said to evil, "Okay, evil, are you finished and satisfied? Great!" Then the Father raises Jesus up from the dead. God had just set a chain of events in process that would ultimately end all suffering, pain, and death.

Jesus is now living in a world free of suffering and evil. He is in heaven with his Father, but he has promised to come again to earth. This time, he will return as the King of Glory and will rule on earth for one thousand years. This period is called the Millennium Reign. We will learn more about this in a later chapter.

The physical resurrection of Jesus over two thousand years ago was the down payment of a plan that will ultimately result in our resurrection and redemption and the renewal of all creation.

God will heal everything. It WILL happen because he began the process when Jesus came to earth. Therefore, the New Testament hope is that, one day, all believers will be with God, and all creation on earth will eventually be renewed when Jesus comes to set up his Kingdom on earth for a millennium reign.

But these things will happen in the future in God's own time. Today, we know that God's Holy Spirit is given to save us, to change us, and to empower us.

Today, the Holy Spirit is now at work ministering to the effects of pain and dealing with evil in our world. One of the ways God will deal with your personal pain is by giving you his Holy Spirit, which will bring healing to your life. This point connects to the next point.

THE HOLY SPIRIT IS BUILDING CHRIST'S CHURCH: Through the work of the cross and Christ's resurrection, Father God has released his Holy Spirit to all believers. God has started the process that will eventually result in the doing away of all evil and suffering. One day when Christ returns, he will wipe away every tear, pain, and suffering. On God's new earth, all creatures will honor each other, and all creation will be in perfect harmony.

Between now and then, God invites all his believers to work with him in the mission of dealing with human rebellion, pain, and so forth. One of our jobs is to deal with the problem of evil, eradicating injustice, poverty, and oppression. We are called to be active in addressing the problem of evil.

Ask God to show you his particular plan for you in this area.

One such proactive organization is called "International Justice Mission," a rescue mission to free young children, boys and girls of all ages, from being sold as sex objects in Indonesia. The Lord put it on my daughter's heart to train young teenagers in her church to raise money by hosting catering for weddings and similar events. All the profits go to International Justice Mission.

God's calling for my daughter has not only helped overseas sex victims by providing extra police, but it has impacted the lives of the young girls in her church. She teaches and demonstrates the principle of living a godly lifestyle to them. These girls are taught not to wear provocative clothing and to refuse to go to places where the Holy Spirit would not be comfortable.

Terrible things are happening in the world today, and innocent people are becoming victims of Satan. People are starving while others are being tortured just for being a Christian. Young girls and even young boys are brutally taken by sex traders and forced to do horrible things for long hours every day. God must weep in heaven when he sees the world today.

We have an incredible calling to deal with these things. So instead of not being able to answer the question about evil, just say to the person, "I'm so glad you have asked me this. I have great news for you. Let me tell you what God has done. Let me tell you about my Jesus and what he wants us to do for him."

This is a long answer to the subject of evil, but the shorter answer might help as well.

Unbelievers and even some believers blame God for bad things, but in fact, the Bible tells us that we have an enemy who is determined to ruin everything God loves. Satan and his wicked demons, along with our own wrong or foolish choices, bring havoc to our lives. Many people also suffer tragedy because of the choices other people have made.

For example, I once heard about two drunken teenagers speeding on a wet night. They failed to negotiate an unexpected sharp curve. Lack of driving experience and alcohol resulted in the car crashing into an oncoming vehicle and killing an innocent driver.

At the man's funeral, his ten-year-old son listened to the minister glibly saying to the mourners that whatever happens, God always works things for good, and they could be sure of that because that is what the Bible promises. He was implying that God had some great plan ahead.

But the devastated young boy decided that day that he never wanted to have anything to do with a God who took his father from him. A root of bitterness rose in his heart, for he was angry—not at the teenagers but at a God who didn't care about his future! That foolish minister did so much damage at the very time that he was actually trying to be helpful.

He had totally misquoted Romans 8:28, which says, "And we know that all things work together for good to those **who love God**, to those who are the called according to His purpose" (emphasis added).

The minister had totally missed the whole context of that verse!

But a Christian friend knew both the local teenagers who had caused the accident. He knew they were rebellious toward all authority and certainly had shown no interest in God. The devil would have encouraged them to drink too much and the untimely curve and prevailing weather conditions played havoc with the driver's lack of experience. This accident was caused by many factors, and God was certainly not one of them.

How many other people have been given the wrong impression about the love of God by others? It's so very important to ask God to give you HIS words for people in situations like this. If you aren't sure what to say, don't make up something but just be a shoulder to cry on.

The world in general has absolutely no idea how much God loves them and what he did to undo the work of the devil when they undermine the goodness of God. The devil never gives up trying to undermine God's goodness to us.

Jesus has promised that he will return to earth, not as a suffering servant but as the mighty Judge of this earth and as the King of Kings! My prayer is that all my readers will rejoice with me on that glorious day.

**Matthew's Comments**
In my Christian life of late, I have been to heaven and spoken to God about suffering on earth and how he feels about it. You can be sure, dear reader, that the suffering of the people in the world is not lost on God. In fact, like a real father on earth, God weeps with all his suffering children, both those that know him and those that do not know him yet.

To give men and women free will was a very expensive thing for God to do. This means that people can essentially do whatever they want. Of course, we have laws, but many people do not care about them. And because people have the choice to do whatever they want to do, many people suffer.

People might wonder, "Where was God when this happened to me?" I have heard this response. "God was in the same place watching you that he was when his own Son was slaughtered on the cross." When you consider that God sees all and is weeping with you, it brings some measure of comfort.

I have had a life filled with suffering, and I have also asked the question, "Why me?" I have seen some pain in my life. You can read more about my life in my book, *His Redeeming Love*.

I feel that my mother has done a very good job of explaining the problem of suffering in this chapter, and I am kind of at a loss of what more to say. I encourage you to read this truth again and again and to share it on Facebook with your friends.

# LESSON 13: A BRIEF SUMMARY OF THE OLD TESTAMENT

God is spirit. Though he is one God, he is made up of the Father, the Son, and the Holy Spirit. He is all-powerful, all knowing, and everywhere at once. He is the Supreme Being, perfect in holiness and love. He yearns for all mankind to become his family. God has many spiritual enemies as Satan and his demons are totally opposed to him. Satan hates all God's creation, especially mankind, who was created in God's image.

From Adam to the time of Moses was approximately two thousand years. In that period, sin existed, but it was not held against man. "For until the law, sin was in the world, but sin is not imputed when there is no law" (Romans 5:13).

But during this period, God made two exceptions of judgment: Noah's flood and Sodom and Gomorrah. In both cases, God had to remove the depravity of unnatural sexual sin. Otherwise, a Jewish virgin might not have ever been found in Israel to give birth to the future Savior.

In Genesis, the first book of the Bible, we read that within six days, God created everything by his spoken word. But Adam and Eve were uniquely handcrafted personally by God. They alone were made in God's own image and were given God's glory and his Holy Spirit, for humans were designed to live forever with him.

God is never surprised by anything because he knows the future. He knew that when he gave Adam the responsibility of being the official caretaker of earth, he would soon lose that authority, and Satan would eventually rule. By disobeying God's command, Adam and Eve lost their former glory and had to leave Paradise. They were no longer innocent and became spiritually dead. Ever since this, everyone is born spiritually dead.

God still longed for a family of his own, so he chose godly Abraham to be the father of a new race of people. Abraham's wife, Sarah, was barren, so at her suggestion, Abraham slept with her maidservant who gave birth to a son named Ishmael. Today, this illegitimate son is the father of the Arab race. In other words, all the Muslims in the world originally came from Ishmael. These people rapidly became the enemy of the Israelites.

Still today, Muslims mostly look down on Christians as well as all Jews. (The term Jew is a name used today for the Israelites.)

God healed Sarah's womb, and her son was named Isaac. He was God's son of promise. The Jewish nation came from Isaac and his wife. From that time right up to the present, Muslims and Jews have been opposed to each other.

Abraham is known by the Jewish people as the father of Judaism. Because of his faith in God's goodness, Abraham is also known by Christians as the father of Christianity. You can read about Abraham's amazing faith in God in Romans 4.

When Isaac was only a young lad, his father was told by God to offer his son as a burnt offering to him. The boy had no idea that he was to become a sacrifice. He innocently said to his father, "Where is the sacrifice, Dad?" To which Abraham said, "God will supply the sacrifice, son." (See Genesis 22.)

Abraham's faith in the goodness of God had not lessened. Just as he was about to stab his son on the altar as a sacrifice to God, he heard God's command to stop. God then supplied a young lamb as the sacrifice, so Isaac's life was spared. God wanted to test Abraham's faith toward him and he passed the test with flying colors. The book of Romans explains Abraham's faith.

Romans 4:17-22 says, "'I have made you a father of many nations' in the presence of Him whom he believed—God, who gives life to the dead and calls those things which do not exist as though they did, who, contrary to hope, in hope believed, so that he became the father of many nations, according to what was spoken, 'So shall your descendants be.' And not being weak in faith, he did not consider his own body, already dead (since he was about a hundred years old,) and the deadness of Sarai's womb.

"He did not waver at the promise of God through unbelief, but was strengthened in faith, giving glory to God and being fully convinced that what He had promised He was also able to perform. And therefore 'it was accounted to him for righteousness.'"

My Bible notes say, "Abram did not deny his or his wife's natural condition, but rather believed God's ability to change circumstances, *by calling those things that did not exist as though they did.* (This verse does not say that God called things that are as though they do not exist.) Faith does not deny the obstacle at hand, but declares that God is greater than the obstacle."[14]

To God, everyone who doesn't have a Jewish mother is called a Gentile. Believing Gentiles are called Christians. But when a Jew responds to Jesus Christ as Lord and Savior of their life, they are called Messianic Jews. The Lord Jesus Christ was God's Messiah (Savior).

In all Jewish history, the most memorable act of God toward his people is called the Passover. This was when God rescued the Israelites from slavery to the Egyptians. God sent an angel of death to each Egyptian home, and the oldest male child was killed. As a result, Pharaoh lost his oldest child. Absolutely devastated, he finally released all the Jewish slaves, but he later changed his mind and chased after them.

But God miraculously parted the Red Sea so that the Israelites could safely cross over to the other side. Then, when the Egyptian army followed in pursuit through the parted waters, God closed the passage mid-way and the Egyptians drowned. (See Exodus 5:1 to

---

[14] Hayford, *The New Spirit-Filled Life Bible.*

14:31.) During that first two thousand years God basically acted in grace toward his chosen people.

Now came a period of God's law that lasted for another two thousand years. This was the period from when God's laws were given right up to the time of Christ. God's chosen people needed to recognize their personal sin and repent. The Israelites compared themselves to others, but they needed to compare themselves to the holiness of God. By comparing themselves to others, Satan would deceive them into thinking that they were so-called good people.

Therefore, while they were wandering in the wilderness after their escape from slavery to the Egyptians, God gave Moses the Ten Commandments. These laws were to reveal to them their utter dependence on God to save them.

God finally had to anoint godly men and women to be his chosen prophets, his representatives to his people. Their task was to convict the Jews of their personal sin and direct them to God. These prophets would hear from God and pass on God's message to his people.

At that time, there were three major Jewish authorities apart from God himself who ruled the Israelites: namely, God's prophet, the high priest, and the king.

For the next two thousand years after the Ten Commandments were given to God's people, God's dealings with Israel radically changed, for the time of God's grace toward his people had ceased. Now for the first time, sin was imputed to man. (To impute something is like buying goods on credit. The payment of the goods is imputed or debited to one's bank account.)

Likewise, sin under the law demands a penalty or payment. In the New Testament, this payment of sin is called wages, and we are told in Romans 3:23 that "the wages of sin is death."

After the Ten Commandments were given to God's people, God basically judged them by the laws he had given them.

Under the law before the cross, man learned that to ignore God's laws brought instant punishment. The people were by nature lovers of themselves and rebelled against authority. Yet God continually longed for a personal relationship with them. They needed to repent and turn from their wicked ways, but his arms were always open to them.

By his laws, God was trying to show his people how weak the flesh was. Man couldn't be good because of the built-in bias to sin they had inherited from Adam. Just as a bowling ball has a resistance bias, so has man without God in him. The law revealed God's holiness but gave no power for obedience. God's intention for the law was only given by God to show man their desperate need of a Savior.

Also, along with the law, God introduced an elaborate sacrifice system to his people. This was to be a temporary measure to cover their sin until Jesus came. The blood sacrifices were a detailed forerunner to the final once and for-all blood sacrifice of Jesus on the cross.

God's prophets were his human representatives. They guided the Jews by their godly wisdom, and at times, they rebuked the people with godly correction. This was to protect them and to keep them as a separate race of people.

Intermarriage with the surrounding nations was totally forbidden because God's anointed one was to come from the Jewish bloodline through the descendants of godly Abraham.

The Jews have been miraculously preserved to this day; they are the oldest surviving race of people in the world. In recent years, many Jews have come to salvation in Christ. Israel will be a major player in the end times. The word Christ or Messiah means God's anointed one."

God's prophets raised up many other prophets in order to teach, guide, and encourage his people. One such prophet was a man named Isaiah who came to power seven hundred years before Christ was born. Isaiah once prophesied, "For unto us a Child is born, unto us a Son is given; and the government will be upon His shoulder, and His name will be called Wonderful, Counselor, Mighty God, Everlasting Father, Prince of Peace. Of the increase of His government (authority) and peace there will be no end, upon the throne of David and over His kingdom, to order it and establish it with judgment and justice, from that time forward, even forever" (Isaiah 9:6-7).

The Jews looked forward to the coming of their mighty God, for they were convinced that he would deliver them from all their enemies, and He would rule forever, and peace would reign.

In the meantime, their prophets guided them with godly wisdom.

The Old Testament is centered on the Jewish people. These people longed for their Messiah to come and rescue them. The Old Testament has great promises for believers today to claim for themselves throughout the thirty-nine separate holy books contained in the Old Testament.

From Christ's death on the cross to today is just over two thousand years. Praise God, today we are no longer under the law because Christ totally fulfilled the whole law on the cross on our behalf.

Therefore like Abraham, today we are privileged to live in a time of God's grace. The Old Testament was God inspired just as the New Testament was written by the guidance of the Holy Spirit of God. The Old Testament sets the stage for the New Testament. Proverbs and Psalms are a particular source of comfort for every Christian today.

The whole Bible is a divine book of history as it is his-story to mankind.

**Matthew's Comments**

The law of God as recorded by Moses might have passed away with the sacrifice of Jesus on the cross, and many seem to think that the Old Testament is largely irrelevant these days. I still have great joy in reading it. I find many helpful promises and great passages to read in the Old Testament.

Many great stories of saints exist in the Old Testament that are full of very helpful lessons. You can benefit greatly by seeing how God dealt with the people of faith through the history of the Bible. I encourage you to take the time to read everything in the Bible. As you spend time in the Christian faith and learn more about the Bible and the men and women of faith and their experiences, your Christian faith will grow stronger.

You can never lose by studying the Bible or by reading passages in the Old Testament, and as I just said, the more that you read and the more that you learn, the stronger your faith will become.

# LESSON 14: A VERY BRIEF SUMMARY OF THE NEW TESTAMENT

Jesus had a miraculous birth, for he did not come from his earthly father's seed but was conceived by the Holy Spirit of God. (See the story in Matthew 1:16-25 and Luke 2:8-20.)

Mary, the mother of Jesus, was a direct descendant of Abraham. The archangel Gabriel came to this young Jewish virgin and then to Joseph her fiancé to say that the Holy Spirit was going to overshadow her physical womb to bring a Savior for mankind into the world.

Therefore, Christ's birth resulted from a supernatural conception by God alone, using a human womb but not a human seed. The inherited sin nature in Mary was bypassed by God's miraculous intervention. This had been prophesied seven hundred years earlier by the prophet Isaiah.

"Therefore the Lord Himself will give you a sign: Behold, the virgin shall conceive and bear a Son, and shall call His name Immanuel" (Isaiah 7:14).

This prophecy came true in the New Testament; Jesus was to be born of the line of King David, and Mary's descendants came from that line. "Then the angel said to her, 'Do not be afraid, Mary, for you have found favor with God. And behold, you will conceive in your womb and bring forth a Son and shall call His name Jesus. He will be great, and will be called the Son of the Highest; and the Lord God will give Him the throne of His father David. And He will reign over the house of Jacob forever, and of His kingdom there will be no end'" (Luke 1:30-33).

At God's appointed time, Jesus was born. He is the grace of God, and he only did what his Father told him to do. To identify with Adam, Jesus had to put aside his divine attributes. He humbly had to live and die as a man, not as God.

Therefore, he experienced tiredness, rejection, pain, and every other human weakness. Jesus was filled with the Holy Spirit just like a Spirit-filled believer is today. His special uniqueness was that he came into the world sinless like Adam. But unlike Adam, Jesus chose to be totally obedient to Father God. If he had sinned just once, he would be a sinner and could not have completed his mission to become the Savior of the world.

Just as there were twelve Jewish tribes in Israel, Jesus chose twelve disciples. Matthew, Mark, Luke, and John each give their personal account of the life, death, and resurrection of Jesus Christ. Matthew had the mind of a Jew. Mark wrote like a news reporter. Luke was a physician and wrote as a scholar. John wrote specifically to all unbelievers.

If you are a new believer, I would advise you not to start reading the Bible at Genesis but to first read the gospel of John. But in all four gospel records, the same Holy Spirit prodded the individual memory of each author and gave them the inspiration to record accurate accounts as they saw them.

The book of Acts reveals the birth of the Christian church. The Bible calls this event Pentecost. Pentecost was, at that time and still is today, the Jewish festival day celebrated fifty days after the Jewish annual Passover Feast.

Since the time of Moses, once every year, the Priest slaughtered a special Passover lamb in the temple at 3:00 p.m. on the Passover Day. This lamb was ceremoniously slaughtered to celebrate God's supernatural deliverance of the Jewish people from four hundred years of slavery to the Egyptians.

But at 3:00 p.m. on this Passover Day, Jesus on the cross outside the city of Jerusalem offered up his Spirit to God at the exact time that the high priest was killing the traditional Passover lamb in the temple.

- Jesus was the perfect Passover Lamb who atoned for all sin for all time.
- Jesus Christ alone sets us free from the slavery of sin and the devil's hold on us.
- Jesus alone gives us eternal life.
- Jesus alone is our great high priest and the King of all Kings.

The disciples had been fearful after the cross, but once the Holy Spirit empowered them for ministry, they became mighty and powerful witnesses. Filled with the Holy Spirit, they brought thousands to a saving belief in the risen Christ.

A highly respected Jewish Pharisee named Saul was highly trained in Jewish law and history. Saul was responsible for the death of early Christian believers because he saw them as heretics to the Jewish faith. But God saw that Saul was a mighty man of faith who was extremely zealous for the things of God.

We read in Acts 9 about Saul's miraculous conversion. God intervened in this man's life in such a life-changing way because God wanted to use Saul's zeal for his own purposes. First, God had to forever change Saul's theology to that of grace. One day when Saul was head-hunting known Christians, he was supernaturally confronted by the risen Christ.

From that time on, instead of preaching the Ten Commandments and all the other laws in the Old Testament, God wanted to use Saul's passion and zeal for legalism and transform his passion to God's favor and grace. First, God changed his name to Paul, and he became a super zealous Christian. God used him to write thirteen of the twenty-seven New Testament books in the Bible.

We must realize that every human being is created by God, but we don't belong to his family until we choose to become a child of God. You become part of the human family at physical birth, but you become part of God's family only by spiritual rebirth. Without rebirth we remain separated from God. Jesus told a teacher of the Law named Nicodemus in John 3:3, "Most assuredly, I say to you, unless one is born again, he cannot see the kingdom of God."

God's invitation to be born again is universal but conditional, for we can only become children of God by faith in Christ alone. "For you are all sons of God through faith in Christ Jesus. For as many of you as were baptized into Christ have put on Christ. There is neither Jew nor Greek, there is neither slave nor free, there is neither male nor female; for you are all one in Christ Jesus" (Galatians 3:26-28).

My Bible notes on Galatians 3:26 say, "When we major in the minors, we end up separated from people who do not look, act, or talk like we do. The only way to overcome this is to be sure that Christ is the first and foremost in our lives and set aside the secondary things that have little ultimate value."[15]

We are to be constantly aware that there is only one way to God, and that is through the Lord Jesus Christ who said, "I am the way, the truth, and the life. No one comes to the Father, except through Me" (John 14:6).

At conversion, every child of God is given amazing gifts: the family name, the family likeness, the family privileges, family intimate access, and family inheritance. As an adopted child, all that Christ has becomes ours! "And if you are Christ's, then you are Abraham's seed, and heirs according to the promise" (Galatians 3:29). "Therefore, you are no longer a slave but a son (or daughter) then an heir of God through Christ" (Galatians 4:7).

What a wonderful identity we have in Christ!

---

[15] Hayford, *The New Spirit-Filled Life Bible*.

Jesus Christ was born pure and lived pure, for he alone is the Savior of the world. He is called the second Adam because, as the only perfect man, he took upon himself the anger of God against the world's collective sin. He died once forever for everyone for all time.

He died on a Friday and rose again early on Sunday. God's love for us and his hatred of sin were both fully satisfied on the cross. Christ's death and resurrection brought in the new covenant of God's grace. This has forever replaced the Old Testament covenant of law.

Out of approximately six thousand years of recorded history:

- Two thousand years was under grace" because God's people were ignorant of their sin.
- Two thousand years was under "the law." God instructed Moses to tell the people his Ten Commandments in order to protect them and to keep them from marrying non-Jews.
- Since the resurrection of Jesus, another two thousand years has passed, and this has been a period of grace. But the devil still causes legalism and not grace to permeate the hearts of many Christians today. These people need a new revelation of God's incredible grace.

Every person's sin on earth has been fully paid for, but each person must personally appropriate grace for themselves. God wants us to choose to believe him and receive his Holy Spirit into our lives before we die. Otherwise, we will be separated from him forever. The devil wants to keep people ignorant of God's answer to sin. Our job on earth is to be Jesus to those we meet so that they will want to be like us. Most importantly, a decision to follow Jesus must be made before our physical death.

Satan and man's wrong choices continually bring suffering to mankind. But if we are born again by the Spirit of God, Satan loses his legal authority over us because we will have a new and merciful Master. We can now claim God's promises and rebuke the devil in the name of Jesus, for he is and will always be God's enemy.

We read in the New Testament that Satan is the god of this world in 2 Corinthians 4:4, but to a born-again believer, Satan is already a defeated foe. Jesus Christ on the cross defeated Satan once for all time. "For in Him (Jesus) dwells all the fullness of the Godhead bodily; and you are complete in Him, who is the head of all principality and power" (Colossians 2:9-10).

The New Testament tells us how to live as Christians and gives us hope for the future. The indwelling Holy Spirit is our comforter, guide, teacher, and our personal friend. He teaches us how to glorify the Lord Jesus Christ and places eternity into our heart. Without his help, no one could live the Christian life.

- Authentic faith does not deny the obstacle at hand but declares that God is greater than the obstacle.
- Faith does not deny that sickness is in the body but declares Jesus's ability to heal the body. The healing faith of a Jewish ruler, Jairus, is recorded in Mark 5:38-43.
- Faith does not deny financial need but acknowledges Jesus's ability to meet our needs. Jesus had no money, but he told Peter to go catch a fish and in its mouth would be enough money to pay the required temple tax. (See Matthew 17:24-27.)

**Matthew's Comments**

I encourage everyone to read the gospels found in the New Testament. I encourage everyone to come to know Jesus as it is only as we come to know Jesus and understand what he taught that we can live a successful Christian life. I have written two books that can give you some insight into the life of Jesus: _Finding Intimacy with Jesus Made Simple_ and _Jesus Speaking Today_. I encourage you to click on these links for the Kindle copies of these books and buy them, and if you are reading the paperback book, I encourage you to look them up on Amazon and purchase copies.

During his preaching ministry, Jesus told stories called parables. These stories had a surface meaning of instruction, and they also had a deeper meaning. I have written a book about these parables of Jesus and how we can live them out and obey them in our own lives today called _The Parables of Jesus Made Simple: Updated and Expanded Edition_. A believer needs to look and act like Jesus does so that we can have an influence on people in the world that don't know him personally. By reading this book on the parables and putting them in practice in our daily lives, we can spread the light of Jesus wherever we go.

The apostles of Jesus had many great lessons to teach us, and we can find their wisdom and instruction in some of the other books of the New Testament. Ask the Holy Spirit to be with you and help you understand the meaning of what they had to say in what they wrote.

# LESSON 15: END TIME EVENTS – PART ONE

The Jewish people longed for their promised Messiah to come and rescue them from Roman rule. According to Zechariah 9:9, their Messiah would be both a conquering King and a suffering Servant. "Rejoice greatly, O daughter of Zion! Shout, O daughter of Jerusalem! Behold, your King is coming to you; He is just and having salvation, lowly and riding on a donkey, a colt, the foal of a donkey (Zechariah 9:9).

This prophecy was actually fulfilled in the New Testament when Jesus made his triumphant entry into Jerusalem on a donkey. The excited people even placed a carpet of palm leaves down for him and proclaimed, "Hosanna! Blessed is He who comes in the name of the LORD! The King of Israel!" (John 12:13). The excited crowd didn't realize that this same Jesus was their suffering servant and would soon be crucified on the cross. But many of the Jewish people turned against Jesus as they wanted a leader who would overthrow the Romans.

The Jewish people believed that their Messiah would wipe out all their enemies and then rule in justice and peace. As such, he would have dominion over all the earth, for Zechariah had also prophesied, "I will cut off the chariot from Ephram and the horse from Jerusalem; The battle bow shall be cut off. He shall speak peace to the nations; His dominion shall be from 'sea to sea, and from the River to the ends of the Earth'" (Zechariah 9:10).

The first part of the prophecy was fulfilled in John 12:12-15 and Matthew 21:1-8. Therefore, we can be assured that one day, King Jesus will majestically return to Jerusalem to set up universal reign and absolute dominion over all the earth.

The two passages in Zechariah 9:9-10 were written around 480 B.C. These verses refer to *two separate events,* one of which Jesus fulfilled by his death and resurrection.

Jesus told his disciples, "In my Father's house are many mansions; if it were not so, I would have told you. I go to prepare a place for you and if I go and prepare a place for you, I will come again and receive you to Myself; that where I am, there you may be also" (John 14:2-3).

Today, Jesus wants our love for him to shine to others because he wants to have a huge family of believers. Today earthly values are rapidly deteriorating, and all manner of evil is escalating at an alarming rate. These things are tangible signs that Jesus will soon come to rescue his believers. At a future date, he will come back as the conquering King of Kings and Lord of Lords to judge all unbelievers.

The rescue of his saints will occur at the rapture, which will take place in the air. It will happen suddenly without warning, in the twinkling of an eye. The second spectacular event will be the awesome day of judgment that will take place on earth after the seven-year tribulation period. This tribulation period might have started already, or perhaps the evil in the world today might just be signs that it will soon start.

The book of Revelation is by far the most difficult book to understand. Only the Holy Spirit can give us spiritual revelation on its message. God himself knows the timing and all the details of end-time prophecies, so I can only explain what I believe will happen from reading my Bible and listening to gifted Christian men and women teach on the subject.

During the seven years of tribulation, every form of evil will rapidly escalate to the point that if God doesn't intervene, no one will be left on earth. God's wrath will be poured out as never before in all the history of man.

As believers in the lordship of Jesus Christ our Savior, we have been promised that we will never experience God's wrath. The Apostle Paul speaks about Jesus who delivers us (every born-again Christian) from the wrath to come (1 Thessalonians 1:10b).

But we are told that "all unbelievers are by nature, children of wrath" (Ephesians 2:3).

When the Lord initially comes in the air, he will come with his mighty angels and like a giant magnet in the sky, he will draw up his Bride from the four corners of the earth and take them to heaven to live with him for all eternity. This event has been the believer's blessed hope since our Lord ascended into heaven at the end of his earthly ministry.

The tribulation on earth will be something that our world has never experienced before. Finally, our Lord Jesus, in all his majesty, power, and glory, will physically set his foot onto the earth, and all evil will be vindicated forever. If he didn't come at that time, no one would probably be left on earth to rescue.

THE RAPTURE OF BELIEVERS: Up to seven years before Jesus sets his foot on earth, this amazing prophecy will be fulfilled. "For the Lord Himself will descend from heaven with a shout, with the voice of an archangel, and with the trumpet of God. And the dead in Christ will rise first. Then we who are alive and remain shall be caught up together with them in the clouds to meet the Lord in the air. And thus we shall always be with the Lord. Therefore comfort one another with these words" (1 Thessalonians 4:16-18).

An example of being snatched up is recorded in Acts 8:26-39. Here we read that, suddenly without warning, the Holy Spirit supernaturally transported the disciple Philip from one location to another so as to bring the Word of God to an Ethiopian man of great authority who had come to Jerusalem to worship.

In a similar way, at the rapture, every born-again believer will be instantly and without warning supernaturally transported from earth to heaven by the power of the Holy Spirit. On the way, our physical body will be changed into a brand new spiritual body. This will be necessary because our present earthly body is seen by God as corrupted, and no corruption of any kind is allowed in heaven. In 1 Corinthians 15:53, we read, "for this corruptible must put on incorruption, and this mortal must put on immortality."

Paul told the believers in the Corinthian church, "Behold, I tell you a mystery: We shall not all sleep, (die) but we shall all be changed—in a moment, in the twinkling of an eye, at the last trumpet. For the *trumpet* will sound, and the dead will be raised incorruptible, and we shall be changed" (1 Corinthians 15:51-52, emphasis added).

After the rapture, all that will be left on the ground will be the clothes we wore, for God will give us his heavenly apparel. If we are alive when Jesus comes at the rapture, we won't experience physical death. Instead, we will instantly receive a glorified body just like Jesus had after his resurrection.

Earlier, I italicized the word trumpet as the last trumpet will usher in the rapture of the Church. "Let no one deceive you by any means; for that Day will not come unless the falling away comes first, and the man of sin is revealed, the son of perdition, who opposes and exalts himself above all that is called God or that is worshiped, so that he sits as God in the temple of God showing himself that he is God" (2 Thessalonians 2:3-4).

This event will occur. Many books have been written on the topic of the second coming. Remember, when the risen Lord suddenly appeared before his disciples in the upper room, *he passed right through the locked door!* His fearful disciples recognized him, *but Jesus told them not to touch him.* They saw the puncture scars on his hands, feet, and side and clearly recognized his loving eyes and caring attitude and knew that he was their wonderful Lord and Savior.

Although Jesus had a resurrected body at the time that was different from their physical body, yet they knew he was their Master. When we are caught up to be with the Lord in the air, we too will have a resurrected body like his. Our body will be fit for heaven and will last for all eternity as it will never grow old.

Pastor Don Kemsley from Coffs Harbour Baptist Church preached a series of sermons on the second coming, but right from the beginning, he wisely encouraged his congregation to focus on the Lord Jesus Christ who is coming rather than on other people's views about the second coming.

I too would advise my readers not to be overly concerned about these things or their sequence but to concentrate on *being like our Lord Jesus Christ to all we meet.* Hebrews 12:2 encourages us to focus on Jesus, for he is the Author and Finisher of our faith. But just like his disciples on earth, today we want to know when Jesus will come back for us.

Jesus told his disciples in Matthew 24:14, "And this gospel of the kingdom will be preached in all the world as a witness to all the nations, and then the end will come."

My Bible notes on Matthew 24:4-14 say, "In warning the disciples against false signs, Jesus sketches the prevailing conditions of their present age, down to the very end and states their continuing task. There will be religious deception, social and political upheavals, natural calamities, disloyalty, and persecution – all of which are precursors of the end times. In the midst of the difficulties, the Lord's followers are to persevere in spreading the gospel."[16]

Even when believers are taken up in the rapture, don't underestimate the power of God. He can still speak to people on earth who have never heard the gospel or who have been hardened to it. He can use the Holy Spirit to speak directly to the person's human spirit or even speak audibly to convict them of sin. We are not to limit God by human reasoning.

In order for anyone to be open to Christianity, God needs to first heal their heart! We were all born sinners, and our hearts were

---

[16] Hayford, *The New Spirit-Filled Life Bible.*

far away from God until HE changed all that. Our prayer today for unbelievers should be, "Change their hearts, Lord!"

Don't limit the power or the love of God by your own unbelief. Satan is causing increasing heartache like never before, and things will only get worse. People need to have hope in the Lord Jesus Christ, for he is the only anchor that will firmly hold.

Jesus knew that evil would increase before he would return to earth. He said, "For then there will be great tribulation that has not been seen since the beginning of the world until this time, no, nor shall ever be. And unless those days were shortened, no flesh would be saved; but for the elect's sake those days will be shortened" (Matthew 24:21-22).

Jesus also told his disciples, "And there will be signs in the sun, in the moon, and in the stars; and on the earth distress of nations, with perplexity, the sea and the waves roaring; men's hearts failing them from fear and the expectation of those things which are coming on the earth, for the powers of the heavens will be shaken. Then they will see the Son of Man coming in a cloud with power and great glory. Now when these things begin to happen, look up and lift up your heads, because your redemption draws near" (Luke 21:25-28).

Apart from meeting the Lord and his angels in heaven, we will meet all our past friends and family members who loved Jesus on earth. We will meet the apostles and other Bible characters, and we will each have a specially built mansion waiting for us to enjoy for all eternity.

Jesus lovingly told his disciples in John 14:1-7, "Let not your heart be troubled; you believe in God, believe also in Me. In My Father's house are many mansions; if it were not so, I would have told you. I go to prepare a place for you. And if I go and prepare a place for you, I will come again and receive you to Myself; that where I am, there you may be also. And where I go you know, and the way you know.

"Thomas said to Him, 'Lord, we do not know where You are going, and how can we know the way?'"

"Jesus said to him, 'I am the way, the truth, and the life. No one comes to the Father except through Me. If you had known Me, you would have known My Father also; and from now on you know Him and have seen Him."

The first part of this verse is absolutely pivotal to the Christian faith as we can only go to heaven by having a personal belief in WHO Jesus really is. He is the Son of God who died for the collective sin of the whole world for all time.

If I am still alive when Jesus comes in the clouds, I will be caught up with him, and midway in the air, I will see my radiant mother, her mother, and my two grown-up daughters coming to greet me, and they will escort me to heaven.

There are three different views about the second coming.

- The pre-tribulation view: Those who hold this view say that Christ will return for his church *before* the seven-year tribulation; thus believers will not experience God's wrath.
- The mid-tribulation view: Those who hold this view believe that the rapture will occur midway through the seven-year tribulation period.
- The post-tribulation view: According to the late Paul E. Little who wrote the book, *Know What You Believe*, Christ's coming for his saints and his revelation (coming with his saints) *is one and the same event*, occurring just *after* the tribulation.

Regardless of when the rapture occurs, we need to conduct our lives so that they reflect the glory of the Kingdom of God to which we belong. Remember the apostle Paul's words. "Much more then, having now been justified by His blood, we shall be saved from wrath through Him" (Romans 5:9). (Personally, I am hanging on to this promise.)

One day, God *will* pour out his wrath against all ungodliness on the earth. At Christ's first coming, his deity was veiled in human flesh. But at the end of the seven-year tribulation, the Lord Jesus Christ will visibly set foot on earth as the mighty Judge and King of the whole world.

Be assured, "For the Father judges no one, but has committed all judgment to the Son that all should honor the Father. He who does not honor the Son does not honor the Father who sent Him" (John 5:22-23).

Despite the differing views, every Christian can assuredly look forward to the indescribable glory and deliverance that will be ours when King Jesus comes. This is our blessed hope—to see Jesus Christ in all his majesty and glory come back again just as the disciples saw him go up into heaven.

**Matthew's Comments**
As a new believer, I suggest that you take some time to mature in your Christian life before you start to discuss end-time events with people. In my experience, no other book of the Bible seems to cause more arguments and contention between people of God then the last book of the Bible.

The fact remains that we serve a God of love and wisdom. No matter what happens or when judgement happens, one thing you can be sure of is that Jesus will be faithful and loyal to those that love and adore him.

A person has to be a very close friend of mine before I will discuss the book of Revelation with them and share my views of what I think will happen and the chronological order of when I believe events will happen.

I think better time can be spent in developing an intimate relationship with Jesus while you are on earth. The closer that you are to Jesus, the more you will be comfortable and at peace, no matter what happens with the world and when it happens. A book that can help you develop a more intimate relationship with Jesus is *7 Keys to Intimacy with Jesus*.

# LESSON 16: END TIME EVENTS – PART TWO

Today, ungodly laws and decisions of men have been passed by unbelieving leaders all over the world. If someone could fix the world's problems, they could easily become a world ruler.

The Bible teaches that one such leader will be the Antichrist. Even on the television news, talk abounds about the possibility of a cashless economy, also foretold in the Bible. Eventually, people worldwide will be forced to receive a personal identity mark on their hand or forehead in order to buy or sell.

The Antichrist will "cause all, both small and great, rich and poor, free and slave, to receive a mark on their right hand or on their foreheads, and that no one may buy or sell except one who has the mark or the name of the beast, or the number of his name. Here is wisdom. Let him who has understanding calculate the number of the beast, for it is the number of a man: His number is 666" (Revelation 13:16-18).

The media will convince unbelievers that people should have a number tattooed on their foreheads or on their arms instead of carrying cash, but Revelation 14:9-11 warns Christians not to take that mark. It would be far better to be homeless or even die of starvation than to take the mark of the beast.

I hope that, in the goodness of God, the rapture will have occurred by that time. But now is the time to draw close to God so that our faith in his goodness toward us grows stronger! Otherwise panic, fear, and hunger might even tempt believers to take the mark.

Just think for a moment what it will be like for people on earth when the rapture occurs. If a Christian is at the wheel of *any vehicle*, without any warning, cars, trains, buses, boats, and planes will be driverless and crash all over the place. Imagine the chaos in hospitals with missing medical staff! How will the media report such an event?

Non-Christian family members will be left behind, wishing that they had taken more notice of the warnings from their loved ones of such an event. Many of these people might come to the Lord. But they will have much suffering and horrific trials to overcome during the tribulation period. They will constantly need to rely on God for wisdom and courage, for people without the mark of the beast will be hunted down like wild animals.

Even down through the centuries, believers of every denomination have had to give up their life for their faith, *yet these willing martyrs will be greatly rewarded in heaven.*

<u>HEAVENLY JUDGMENT:</u> After physical death, every believer will be personally judged for his or her attitudes and actions since salvation. This judgment is for Christians and is called the judgment at the bema seat of Christ. It will take place at the judgment seat of Christ.

At this judgment, sin will not be the issue because Christ paid for our sin. Here will be determined our rewards or our loss of rewards and our eternal position and responsibility in heaven. The following verses talk about this event. "For the time has come for judgment to begin at the house of God; and if it begins with us first, what will be the end of those who do not obey the gospel of God?" (1 Peter 4:17).

"For we must all appear before the judgment seat of Christ, that each one may receive the things done in the body, according to what he has done, whether good or bad" (2 Corinthians 5:10).

"And now, little children, abide in Him, that when He appears, we may have confidence and not be ashamed before Him at His coming" (1 John 2:28).

"Be ready, for the Son of Man is coming at an hour you do not expect" (Matthew 24:44).

Now is the time to work with the Holy Spirit to control our thought life. "Finally, brethren, whatever things are true, whatever things are noble, whatever things are just, whatever things are pure, whatever things are lovely, whatever things are of good report, if there is any virtue and if there is anything praiseworthy—meditate on these things" (Philippians 4:8).

Ask yourself these questions:

- Does my speech add value to God and others?
- Do I hold offenses toward others, refusing to forgive them?
- Do I aim for unity of spirit and show compassionate love?
- Is criticism more natural than praise? Am I focused on self or on God?

Matthew 12:36 shows us that our words are important, for they can build up or pull down other people. However, we are not to live in regret because all our words have been washed in the blood of the Lamb.

Jesus doesn't want us to waste our gifts, talents, or opportunities. But our *achievements* are not rewarded but rather our faithfulness in using God's blessings. What we may try to hide now will be openly revealed then. Our life since salvation will be assessed by what our heart motives were as seen by God.

Faith is invisible, but the results are clearly seen. Our heart determines why we do things. Correct belief builds faith; unsound belief results in fleshly works that will burn up on that day. "For no other foundation can anyone lay than that which is laid, which is Jesus Christ. Now if anyone builds on this foundation with gold, silver, precious stones, wood, hay, straw, each one's work will become clear; for the Day will declare it, because it will be revealed by fire; and the fire will test each one's work, of what sort it is. If anyone's work which he has built on endures, he will receive a reward. If anyone's work is burned, he will suffer loss; but he himself will be saved, yet so as through fire" (Corinthians 3:11-15).

This tells us that all fleshly works, works done in our own strength, are classed as combustible materials, leaving the person only with basic salvation. But all work done in the power of the Holy Spirit is non-flammable; they last forever and will be eternally rewarded on that day.

Jesus predicted such things as false prophets, wars, earthquakes, violence, the depravity of man, famines, broken agreements, persecution, and more as the beginnings of the end leading to his return. Keep your thoughts focused on Jesus rather than being overly worried about the problems of this world. Now is the time to draw close to God in every way you can. Be Jesus to others and know that he is our constant strength and mighty protector.

Rest in the fact that God is well able to care for his own kids. See Psalm 37:5, Psalm 55:22, Proverbs 16:3, Romans 8:35-39, and 1 Peter 5:7 to name just a few promises of God.

Keep focused on obedience to God's revealed will and rest in the promise of Jesus in John 14:1-3. "Let not your heart be troubled; you believe in God, believe also in Me. In My Father's house are many mansions; if it were not so, I would have told you. I go to prepare a place for you. And if I go and prepare a place for you, I will come again and receive you to Myself; that where I am, there you may be also."

None of us really know when the rapture will happen, so if we live as if Jesus was coming today, we will give urgent attention to what matters most to God. View life in the light of eternity, and you will maintain the right perspective

THE SECOND STAGE OF CHRIST'S RETURN: This will happen when the Lord Jesus Christ *physically returns to earth as king and judge, and every eye shall see him.* Unlike the rapture, his return to earth will not happen secretly but in open view. He will first rescue any new believers and then the door of grace will be shut. Persecuted Christians saved after the rapture will rejoice at his coming, but unbelievers will want the ground to swallow them up on that awesome day. (See Revelation 19:11-16). What an awesome day that will be; Jesus, King of Kings and Lord of Lords, will thrill the hearts of the believers on earth and will absolutely terrify everyone else.

The one-thousand-year millennium reign will begin. First Satan will be bound and thrown into a bottomless pit where he can no longer deceive anyone for a thousand years (Revelation 20:1-4). King Jesus will rule the whole earth from Jerusalem (Revelation 20:6). Even though Satan will be bound up in a pit, people will be born during this thousand years of peace who will rebel against the ruling and visible Christ. At the end of the Millennium, Satan and his demons will be destroyed, together with all the rebels on earth.

All the ungodly dead people going back to Adam will then be resurrected to face the final judgment. Just like at the rapture, the power of Christ's command will supernaturally reassemble the original human molecules of past unbelievers. Then Christ will resurrect these people for judgment, and they will all be found guilty. This judgment is called the great white throne judgment (See Revelation 20:11-15.) (No Christian will be part of this final judgment.)

The once sacrificial Lamb of God will now rule as the Lion of Judah and the Lord of Lords. King Jesus will majestically sit on his throne as the awesome judge, ordained and appointed by the Father to exercise eternal justice against sin. God's mercy to man was demonstrated on the cross, but his *justice now will reign!* (See Acts 17:31a, John 5:22 and Revelation 20:12-15.)

After the great white throne judgment, this present earth will be burned up, and a wonderful and perfect new earth and heavens will be established. (See 2 Peter 3:9-14 and Revelation 21:1.)

I believe that God has chosen to veil the details of the second coming because he wants us to get on with the job he has appointed to us—to be a minister of reconciliation to draw others to Jesus (2 Corinthians 5:18-21). We have a wonderful Savior, an awesome gospel message, and truly amazing promises of God.

"God demonstrates His own love toward us, in that while we were still sinners, Christ died for us. Much more then, having now been justified by His blood, we shall be saved from wrath through Him" (Romans 5:8-9). The Jerusalem Bible states, "Having died to make us righteous—is it likely that He would now fail to save us from God's anger?"

A paraphrase of Romans 5:8-9 follows. As a sinner, Christ died for you. Therefore, certainly as His child, you will be saved from His wrath, because you have already been justified by His blood. Paul later said in 1 Thessalonians 1:10, "And to wait for His Son from heaven, whom He raised from the dead, even Jesus who delivers us from the wrath to come."

NOTE: The subject of end-times events is extremely controversial, and for that very reason, the devil would love the topic to become a road block to our growth in Christ. He wants us to be side-tracked from doing what is really important to God. We are meant to make disciples for Jesus by becoming Christ-like in our day-to-day relationships. Head knowledge with no action will puff us up with pride, and pride is the root of all evil.

The following words are in the final "Truth and Action" section of my Bible. "Spiritual victory is something we enter into. Jesus Christ has already won the victory through His death, burial, and resurrection. Conduct spiritual warfare, on the basis of Jesus' shed blood and through the declaration that He died for your sins and rose again for your justification. Love the Lord more than life itself."[17]

---

[17] Hayford, *The New Spirit-Filled Life Bible*.

As I close, let me share one final note with you. The message we are to preach—not so much by our words, but more importantly, by our actions toward others—is that we are cleansed by the blood of Jesus and justified in his sight. Let Christ be seen in you even when things go wrong. God wants to go on expanding heaven for all the many billions of people who will eventually live there one day.

**Matthew's Comments**

So now as a reader, you have read quite a bit about Christian discipleship. Along the way, I have been adding a little to what my mother has written. I hope that you have enjoyed what she has had to say and that my regular readers have enjoyed what I have had to say in each chapter, no matter how little it has been.

My mother wrote about the Christian judgment when we receive rewards for the work that we have done on earth. We must live our lives on earth as Christians in such a way that we really bless and encourage others. I have written a book on how you can live your life in a rewarding way called *Living for Eternity*. I encourage you to buy it, read it, and apply it.

# I'd love to hear from you

One of the ways that you can bless me as a writer is by writing an honest and candid review of my book on Amazon. I always read the reviews of my books, and I would love to hear what you have to say about this one.

Before I buy a book, I read the reviews first. You can make an informed decision about a book when you have read enough honest reviews from readers. One way to help me sell this book and to give me positive feedback is by writing a review for me. It doesn't cost you a thing but helps me and the future readers of this book enormously.

To read my blog, request a life-coaching session, request your own personal prophecy, request a visit to heaven, or to receive a personal message from your angel, you can also visit my website at http://personal-prophecy-today.com All of the funds raised through my ministry website will go toward the books that I write and self-publish.

You can also request a trip to heaven with Robin Gann. You can find her contact information on my website.

To write to me about this book or to share any other thoughts, please feel free to contact me at my personal email address at survivors.sanctuary@gmail.com

You can also friend request me on Facebook at Matthew Robert Payne. Please send me a message if we have no friends in common as a lot of scammers now send me friend requests.

You can also do me a huge favor and share this book on Facebook as a recommended book to read. This will help me and other readers.

# How to Sponsor a Book Project

If you have been blessed by this book, perhaps you might consider sponsoring a book for me. It normally costs me between $1,500 and $2,000 or more to produce each book that I write, depending on the length of the book.

If you seek the Holy Spirit about financing a book for me, I know that the Lord would be eternally grateful to you. Consider how much this book has blessed you and then think of hundreds or even thousands of people who would be blessed by a book of mine. As you are probably aware, the vast majority of my books are ninety-nine cents on Kindle, which proves to you that book writing is indeed a ministry for me and not a money-making venture. I would be very happy if you supported me in this.

If you have any questions for me or if you want to know what projects I am currently working on that your money might finance, you can write to me at survivors.sanctuary@gmail.com and ask me for more information. I would be pleased to give you more details about my projects.

You can sow any amount to my ministry by simply sending me money via the PayPal link at this address: http://personal-prophecy-today.com/support-my-ministry/

You can be sure that your support, no matter the amount, will be used for the publishing of helpful Christian books for people to read.

# Other Books by Matthew Robert Payne

The Prophetic Supernatural Experience

Prophetic Evangelism Made Simple

Your Identity in Christ

His Redeeming Love: A Memoir

Writing and Self-Publishing Christian Nonfiction

Coping with your Pain and Suffering

Living for Eternity

Jesus Speaking Today

Great Cloud of Witnesses Speak

My Radical Encounters with Angels

Finding Intimacy with Jesus Made Simple

My Radical Encounters with Angels: Book Two

A Beginner's Guide to the Prophetic

Michael Jackson Speaks from Heaven

7 Keys to Intimacy with Jesus

Conversations with God: Book 1

Optimistic Visions of Revelation

Conversations with God: Book 2

Finding Your Purpose in Christ

Influencing your World for Christ: Practical Everyday Evangelism

Deep Calls unto Deep: Answering Questions on the Prophetic

My Visits to the Galactic Council of Heaven

The Parables of Jesus Made Simple: Updated and Expanded Edition

Great Cloud of Witnesses Speak: Old and New

Walking under an Open Heaven

A Message from My Angel: Book 1

Interviews with the Two Witnesses: Enoch and Elijah Speak

Gaining Freedom from Sex Addictions: Breaking Free of Pornography and Prostitutes

Mary Magdalene Speaks from Heaven: A Divine Revelation

Princess Diana Speaks from Heaven: A Divine Revelation

How to Hear God's Voice: Keys to Conversational Two-Way Prayer

Apostle John Speaks from Heaven: A Divine Revelation

What I Believe

Great Cloud of Witnesses Speak: God's Generals

Apostle Peter Speaks from Heaven: A Divine Revelation

You can find my published books on my Amazon author page here: http://tinyurl.com/jq3h893

Upcoming Books:

King David Speaks from Heaven: A Divine Revelation

# About Matthew Robert Payne

Matthew was raised in a Baptist church and was led to the Lord at the tender age of eight. He has experienced some pain and darkness in his life, which has given him a deep compassion and love for all people.

Today, he's a founding member and admin of a Facebook group called "Prophetic Training Group," and he invites you to join him there. Matthew has a commission from the Lord to train up prophets and to mentor others in the Christian faith. He does this through his Facebook posts and by writing relevant books on the Christian faith.

God has commissioned him to write at least fifty books in his life, and he spends his days writing and earning the money to self-publish. You can support him by donating money at http://personal-prophecy-today.com or by requesting any of the other services available through his ministry website.

Recently, the Lord has put it on his heart to start his own publishing company for other people's books. It is going to be called Christian Book Publishing USA. It is Matthew's hope to help some people self-publish their books in the future.

It is Matthew's prayer that this book has blessed you, and he hopes it will lead you into a deeper and more intimate relationship with God.

# End notes

[1] "Turn Your Eyes upon Jesus," Timeless Truths, Accessed January 19, 2018, http://library.timelesstruths.org/music/Turn_Your_Eyes_upon_Jesus. [
2] Andrew Wommack and Don Krow, The Complete Discipleship Evangelism Course: Condensed Version and Workbook. (Europe: Andrew Wommack Ministries, 2007), 53-54. [
3] Jack Hayford, et al., New Spirit-Filled Life Bible, (Nashville: Thomas Nelson Bibles, 2013).
[4] Hayford, The New Spirit-Filled Life Bible.
[5] Hayford, The New Spirit-Filled Life Bible.
[6] "Baptizo," Bible Study Tools, Accessed February 5, 2018, https://www.biblestudytools.com/lexicons/greek/nas/baptizo.html.
[7] Hayford, The New Spirit-Filled Life Bible.
[8] Hayford, The New Spirit-Filled Life Bible.

[9] Hayford, The New Spirit-Filled Life Bible.
10] Andrew Wommack and Don Krow, The Complete Discipleship Evangelism Course: Condensed Version and Workbook. [
11] "Genesis 17 – God Reaffirms the Covenant," Enduring Word, David Guzak, accessed February 5, 2018, https://enduringword.com/bible-commentary/genesis-17/ [
12] Hayford, The New Spirit-Filled Life Bible.
[13] Hayford, The New Spirit-Filled Life Bible. [
14] Hayford, The New Spirit-Filled Life Bible. [
15] Hayford, The New Spirit-Filled Life Bible.
[16] Hayford, The New Spirit-Filled Life Bible.
[17] Hayford, The New Spirit-Filled Life Bible.

Payne, June. Christian Discipleship Made Simple (Kindle Locations 2751-2774). Christian Book Publishing USA. Kindle Edition.

www.ingramcontent.com/pod-product-compliance
Lightning Source LLC
Chambersburg PA
CBHW052034070526
44584CB00016B/2042